NOW AND AT THE HOUR
OF OUR DEATH

NIKOLAS T. NIKAS, M.A., J.D.
BRUCE W. GREEN, TH.M., J.D.

NOW AND AT THE HOUR OF OUR DEATH

*Making Moral Decisions
at the End of Life*

IGNATIUS PRESS   SAN FRANCISCO

While the authors are licensed attorneys, this book is in no way intended to offer legal advice of any kind. To the extent that any question or answer in this book raises, intersects with, or suggests a legal issue, the authors respectfully direct the reader to seek licensed and competent legal counsel from their own state or other relevant legal jurisdiction.

Cover art and design by John Herreid

© 2024 by Nikolas T. Nikas and Bruce W. Green
All rights reserved
ISBN 978-1-62164-225-1 (PB)
ISBN 978-1-64229-250-3 (eBook)
Library of Congress Control Number 2023949790
Printed in the United States of America ∞

To Melinda and Debra, our faithful companions and the pillars of our support in an inhospitable world.

Sancta Maria, Mater Dei, ora pro nobis peccatóribus, nunc et in hora mortis nostrae. Amen.

You turn man back to the dust,
and say, "Turn back, O children of men!"
For a thousand years in your sight
are but as yesterday when it is past,
or as a watch in the night.

You sweep men away; they are like a dream,
like grass which is renewed in the morning:
in the morning it flourishes and is renewed;
in the evening it fades and withers.

So teach us to number our days
that we may get a heart of wisdom.
Return, O LORD! How long?
Have pity on your servants!

Satisfy us in the morning with your mercy,
that we may rejoice and be glad all our days.
Let the favor of the Lord our God be upon us,
and establish the work of our hands upon us,
yes, establish the work of our hands.

Psalm 90:3–6, 12–14, 17

CONTENTS

Part III: The Church's Teaching
on Death and Specific
End-of-Life Decisions

Part IV: Hindrances to Moral
Decision-Making at the
End of Life

Part V: How God Sees Us and the
Significance of This Vision
for End-of-Life Decisions

Part VI: Happiness and Its Relation
to Moral Decision-Making

Part VII: The Moral Law and
Moral Decision-Making

Part VIII: Preparing and Planning for Serious Illness and the End of Life

INTRODUCTION

Death is the one constant and undisputed reality of the human condition. The circumstances of our respective deaths will be as diverse as the readers of this book. Some of us will die suddenly, in an accident, during an acute medical crisis, or simply, quietly in our sleep. Although an abrupt death leaves loved ones behind in shock and sorrow, it eliminates the need to make difficult moral decisions about end-of-life medical care. Other deaths, however, do often raise serious medical and ethical questions. Due to advancements in medicine, some of us will die slowly, whether from a chronic or acute disease, the delayed or lingering effects of an accident, or old age. Modern medicine's ability to sustain and extend life far beyond what was possible just a few generations ago has created the uniquely modern question of whether specific medical treatments are morally appropriate. For Catholics, as we will see, moral questions are understood according to the principle that all the acts of a person, if done consciously and freely, either lead him nearer to his ultimate end and supreme happiness (life with God) or lead him farther away from it (see QQ. 80–86 for a full treatment of this recurring idea).

The success of modern technology and medical advancements raises new moral problems.[1] Also, a culture's

[1] Congregation for the Doctrine of the Faith, *Declaration on Euthanasia* (May 5, 1980), introduction: "Medicine has increased its capacity to cure and to prolong life in particular circumstances, which sometimes give rise to moral problems."

prevailing psychology informs its medicine, and modern psychology tends to view man as nothing more than a physical or material thing.[2] Such an understanding leads inevitably to medical advancements untethered from any concern for the eternal soul of man and medical interventions that consequently take no thought for the "possibilities for evil" that can flow from medical progress.[3]

End-of-life decision-making is more difficult today than ever for at least three reasons. First, the Catholic Church's teachings on the principles that govern such decisions are not well known. Many Catholics have an inadequate foundation and framework for recognizing and analyzing the moral problems arising from medical advancements.

Second, advancements in technology have made an ethical understanding of modern medical science increasingly difficult for the average layperson. Even well-educated people usually lack a basic familiarity with common medical terminology, not to mention relevant medical diagnoses

[2] Chad Ripperger, SMD, *Introduction to the Science of Mental Health* (Keenesburg, CO: Sensus Traditionis Press, 2013), 6–7. Ripperger cites John Watson, "Psychology as the Behaviorist Views It", in *Classics in Psychology*, ed. Thorne Shipley (New York: Philosophical Library, 1961), 798: "It [modern psychology] originally began with the conception that man was a composite of body and soul and later psychologists began the move away from this notion until recently man is viewed as a purely material being no different from an animal."

[3] The Catholic Church has cautioned that the absence of a moral compass directing the progress of some modern technologies and medical interventions has led to a disregard for the dignity of man and his ultimate purpose and happiness. Pope Benedict XVI alluded to this possibility when he stated: "Without doubt, it [progress] offers new possibilities for good, but it also opens appalling possibilities for evil—possibilities that formerly did not exist. We have all witnessed the way in which progress, in the wrong hands, can become and has indeed become a terrifying progress in evil. If technical progress is not matched by corresponding progress in man's ethical formation, in man's inner growth (cf. *Eph* 3:16; *2 Cor* 4:16), then it is not progress at all, but a threat for man and for the world." Benedict XVI, encyclical letter *Spe salvi* (Saved in Hope) (November 30, 2007), no. 22.

and treatment options. Thus, the average person is an easy mark for authoritative-sounding medical assertions, even immoral ones, in the name of science.

Finally, end-of-life decision-making is sometimes difficult because it requires the use of what the Catholic Church calls "prudential judgment"—that is, the use of our practical reasoning to understand and apply the correct moral principles to specific concrete situations to reach proper moral conclusions.[4] Prudential judgment is not always easy to exercise for simple moral questions, much less when we are faced with our mortality or in the emotionally wrenching context of a loved one's dying (see especially QQ. 87–101 for more on how we use our reason with regard to morality).

It is difficult to overstate the threat that this combination of advancing medical technology and a failure to understand the principles of moral decision-making poses to mankind at this point in history. Abortion has been a special threat to life in the womb for the past half century, but the threats facing the aging, ill, and dying in the world today[5] carry the added potential that the victim will also be the perpetrator. That is, abortion poses a danger to the lives but not the souls of its tiny victims; but morally wrong end-of-life decisions can also imperil the soul.

---

[4] Thomas Aquinas, *Summa Theologiae*, trans. Fathers of the English Dominican Province (Notre Dame, IN: Ave Maria Press, 1948), II-II, q. 47, art. 2. All *Summa Theologiae* quotes in this text will come from this edition. Aquinas writes that prudence is "right reason applied to action" (quoting Aristotle).

[5] Typically, those age sixty and older, whose worldwide population the World Health Organization projects will double (to 2.1 billion) by 2050. Of this number, the portion of persons aged eighty years or older is expected to triple between 2020 and 2050 to reach 426 million. "Ageing and Health", World Health Organization, October 1, 2021, https://www.who.int/news-room/fact-sheets/detail/ageing-and-health.

Any approach to making good decisions in serious illness and at the end of life should consider the threats that come from the intersection of medical advancements and a general decline in morality and moral formation, as well as the more timeless problems of an excessive fear of suffering (see especially QQ. 61–65) and a reluctance to remember and embrace our mortality.

These matters must be considered, decided, and prepared for now. Otherwise, as Saint Robert Bellarmine notes, a person may be "compelled, when unprepared, oppressed by disease, and scarcely possessed of reason, to give an account of those things on which when in health, he had perhaps never once reflected".[6] Given recent medical and technological advancements, a growing number of us will face the possibility of dying in a hospital or hospice setting, sometimes after prolonged illness, perhaps over-medicalized—which contributes to dying poorly[7]—and after numerous medical interventions of doubtful morality and questionable effectiveness. Many of us will be faced with an abundance of well-intended medical options that actually dehumanize life and undercut true human dignity. Inevitably, we or our loved ones will be faced with these confusing options when our decision-making powers are not at their peak. These possibilities highlight the need for

[6] Robert Bellarmine, *The Art of Dying Well*, trans. John Dalton (London: Richardson and Son, 1845), preface, http://www.saintsbooks.net/books/St.%20Robert%20Bellarmine%20-%20The%20Art%20of%20Dying%20Well.html. This is a complete English translation that contains the practical and moving preface by Bellarmine.

[7] See L. S. Dugdale, *The Lost Art of Dying Well: Reviving Forgotten Wisdom* (New York: HarperCollins, 2020), 6. Dugdale cites the Harvard study by T. A. Balboni et al., "Provision of Spiritual Support to Patients with Advanced Cancer by Religious Communities and Associations with Medical Care at the End of Life", *JAMA Internal Medicine* 173, no. 12 (2013). Dugdale notes that the Harvard study indicates that some people of religious faith tend to over-medicalize when facing serious illness and death.

sound moral formation long before we die and deep trust in the goodness of God throughout our lives.

While this book is not intended as a technical work on medicine, theology, philosophy, or law, it will touch on all those disciplines. We aim to set forth a clear and concise summary of the Catholic Church's moral tradition surrounding end-of-life decision-making and shed light on the practical process of ethical decision-making in general. We intend the book to serve as a helpful guide during what is perhaps life's most critical period—that stage of life when our primary duty is shifting to the contemplation of the four last things: death, judgment, heaven, and hell. To that end, the suggestions below on how to use the book may prove helpful.

It bears emphasizing that few things in this book are the authors' original ideas. Almost every question calls for a technical, sometimes authoritative, answer that not only cannot be but ought not to be original. We are not likely to improve upon the ideas of Saint Augustine and others who have gone before us and explained a concept or teaching better than we can, so we have been careful to attribute the ideas we discuss to their source. Any failure to do so is an unintentional oversight, for which we ask forgiveness in advance. Moreover, our intention is to be clear in dealing with these matters of the soul, and we willingly accept the correction of any imprecise terminology we have used.

Two Premises That Undergird the Book

This book is built on two foundational ideas that inform everything we have written. The first is that thinking about end-of-life decisions is not a morbid exercise. It is fundamentally about happiness, and this book is about happiness—happiness not only at the hour of our death but happiness now.

By happiness, we don't mean affability, that virtue that helps us make friends. Nor do we mean the attainment of strength, beauty, pleasure, or even physical health. These earthly goods wax and wane, and they disappear at death. Instead, happiness is to be found in the good of a person's soul.[8] The only thing that can make us truly happy involves something outside ourselves: only by union with God can a man be truly happy, living forever in joyous, face-to-face communion with him. He is the sovereign good that makes us happy.

We are created in such a way that we desire happiness more than anything else, yet final and perfect happiness can be found in God alone (see Q. 82). Happiness is not available to man on his own terms but comes by being united to God through Jesus Christ. There are many beneficial spiritual books by authors more qualified to help a person enter and enjoy this happiness through an intimate relationship with Jesus Christ. We mention several in Appendix III of the book.

Making moral decisions at the end of life is not just about navigating serious illness and having a peaceful death; it is about attaining ultimate happiness. Saint Robert Bellarmine wrote, "A good death depends upon a good life."[9] Simply put, our end of happiness in God does not come about by one decision as death approaches; it comes about

[8] Walter Farrell, O.P., and Martin J. Healy, *My Way of Life: The Summa Simplified for Everyone* (Brooklyn, NY: Confraternity of the Precious Blood, 1952), 158–59.

[9] Robert Bellarmine, S.J., *The Art of Dying Well: Or, How to Be a Saint, Now and Forever* (Manchester, NH: Sophia Institute Press, 2021), 5. This Sophia Institute Press edition is a modern republication of the original, and presents Book 1 of the original work, except Chapter 17, which is taken from Book 2. The fuller online version of this book is referenced above.

by faith, hope, and cooperation with God every moment of every day to the end of our lives on earth. Our ultimate happiness at the hour of our death and beyond will be the result of our pursuit and enjoyment of happiness on earth right now.

Having been created in the image of God, with intellect and free will, man has as his ultimate end the everlasting happiness produced by face-to-face communion with God in heaven. Life on earth is a journey through this world of time and trouble to the timeless and perfect beatitude of the vision of God.

The key to each person's reaching this final destiny in heaven lies in the proper use of his freedom, meaning his control over his own acts (decisions). Men use their God-given freedom to make innumerable choices throughout life that move them either closer to true happiness and their ultimate end or farther away from it. This book is about some of those choices that occur, usually after a long life, when people are sick and when they are unprepared to make such decisions because they gave them no thought when they were young and healthy.

There are forces that oppose one's freedom to make good moral choices now and at the end of life, and these enemies come from both within and without. The enemy of free will from without is force, the weakest of freedom's enemies. That is not the focus of this book. Instead, we address the perilous internal enemies of man's freedom: fear, concupiscence (strong desires that override reason), and ignorance. These enemies are all within and must often be called to our attention and warned against.

In emphasizing threats to this internal freedom, we address how to make decisions that tend toward happiness on earth, which prepares us to make difficult and complex end-of-life decisions in our most vulnerable hour.

All men and women hope to enter "consummate and everlasting happiness",[10] the summation of a long life devoted to God and family. As Cicero noted, aging does not have to be a burden.[11] Making morally good choices in old age, like happiness, depends upon having the formation and inner resources to know what to do now and at the moment of our death.

The second premise that undergirds this book is that end-of-life decisions are becoming over-medicalized and technologically driven to the detriment of more important things.[12] We do not mean that medicine and technology are unimportant—only that they are less important than matters of the soul (see QQ. 34–35). It is easy to slip into the assumption that end-of-life decisions are merely about having the latest medical interventions and technologies available. This is a false and harmful belief. The soul always takes priority over the body.[13]

[10] Thomas Aquinas, "Prayer of St. Thomas Aquinas", in Francis Xavier Lasance, *The Prisoner of Love: Instructions and Reflections on Our Duties towards Jesus in the Most Holy Sacrament of the Altar* (New York: Benziger Brothers, 1919), 330, https://archive.org/stream/prisonerofloveinoolasa/prisonerofloveinoolasa_djvu.txt.

[11] Cicero, *On Old Age and On Friendship*, trans. Frank O. Copley (Ann Arbor, MI: University of Michigan Press, 1980), 4–5.

[12] See *The Art of Dying: A New Annotated Translation*, trans. Columba Thomas (Philadelphia: The National Catholic Bioethics Center, 2021), 3. These are the words of translator Brother Columba Thomas, OP, MD, in the introduction to a new annotated translation of this outstanding text of the Middle Ages known as *ars moriendi* (*The Art of Dying*). This work may be the best Catholic handbook on dealing with serious illness and dying. The National Catholic Bioethics Center, whose general work on bioethics the authors recommend as a critical resource, has served modern Catholics by publishing this new annotated translation, to which the authors will refer in this book, particularly in Part VIII.

[13] *The Art of Dying*, 17. See also *Catechism of the Catholic Church*, no. 997: "In death, the separation of the soul from the body, the human body decays and the soul goes to meet God, while awaiting its reunion with its glorified body. God, in his almighty power, will definitively grant incorruptible life to our bodies by reuniting them with our souls, through the power of Jesus' Resurrection."

Any approach to making decisions at the end of life must be balanced, considering medical and technological advancements in the context of the concrete circumstances of persons involved. Still, it must do so without losing sight of the fact that the condition and the end of the soul are more important than the body. Thus, this book includes questions and answers that go beyond the context of medicine and technology. This is appropriate because end-of-life decisions are about happiness now and at the hour of our death, which necessarily involves the soul.

Finally, every book is written for a particular audience. This book is directed mainly at Catholics—thus the recurring appeal to the "teachings of the Catholic Church", which is Catholic shorthand for the body of authoritative Catholic doctrine that comes from the natural law, philosophy, biblical exegesis, and theology developed over two thousand years of the Church's history. The Catholic Church's teachings on morality and end-of-life issues are rooted in the natural law, written on the hearts of all to provide *universal and authoritative moral guidance to every person*. We thus hope and pray that this book will also be well received by our non-Catholic friends who seek to make good end-of-life decisions. May God give us all the courage to face our humanity and follow the light he gives us.

A General Description of the Book and How to Profitably Use It

This kind of book comes together in pieces. It has grown from real-life experiences, a little at a time, and from questions, objections, and dissents during debates in America's law schools, medical schools, and universities, as well as presentations to Catholic laity in countless parishes around the country. The book's question-and-answer format does not lend itself to a perfectly interconnected reading experience—one paragraph and topic leading organically into the next toward a final and cohesive thesis. Instead, the format is patterned after the way that the issues have been raised to the authors over the years: one at a time, often in rapid succession.

Making end-of-life decisions can be difficult for the average person without training in medicine, philosophy, theology, and ethics. The goal of this book is to provide uncomplicated guidance in understanding complicated issues. Many terms and phrases are defined within the questions discussing them, but for further clarity, Appendix IV is an alphabetical list of terms with their definitions.

The work contains eight parts with varying numbers of practical questions:

Part I: Why This Book Is Important (Questions 1–8). This part defines "end of life" and "end-of-life decisions" and explains what morality has to do with decision-making and why people should read the book.

Part II: What the Church Teaches about Caring for the Seriously Ill and Dying (Questions 9–33). This part addresses the Church's teaching on "hot-button issues" related to caring for the seriously ill, explains the means of determining which medical treatments and interventions are morally obligatory and which are optional, and discusses the role of painkillers and sedatives.

Part III: The Church's Teaching on Death and Specific End-of-Life Decisions (Questions 34–48). This part discusses the nature of death and how it is determined, as well as the Church's teaching regarding physician-assisted suicide and euthanasia.

Part IV: Hindrances to Moral Decision-Making at the End of Life (Questions 49–71). Many popularly held beliefs about end-of-life issues are false or misunderstood and thus are hindrances to moral decision-making in a health crisis. This part addresses the most common misconceptions, such as ideas about the role of conscience, fear of suffering, dying alone and penniless, "death with dignity", being a burden, and personal autonomy.

Part V: How God Sees Us and the Significance of This Vision for End-of-Life Decisions (Questions 72–79). One cannot understand moral decision-making without understanding the nature and end of man, the duties he owes to God, his condition in the world, and why these are critical to making right decisions at the end of life. This part addresses these matters.

Part VI: Happiness and Its Relation to Moral Decision-Making (Questions 80–86). Although it appears later in the book, this part explains one of the book's major premises: that man desires happiness more than anything, which drives his decision-making. This part introduces the reader to how happiness is related explicitly to end-of-life decisions.

Part VII: The Moral Law and Moral Decision-Making (Questions 87–101). This part explains the authoritative standard that guides the Church and individuals in moral decision-making, the elements of a moral decision, and why certain acts and decisions are always morally evil.

Part VIII: Preparing and Planning for Serious Illness and the End of Life (Questions 102–123). This final part deals with how to prepare the soul for illness and death, including specific practical decisions and preparations that can be made in advance.

Appendix I: The Principle of Double Effect and Its Application in End-of-Life Decisions. Question 31 introduces the relevance of this appendix, which briefly explains the Church's use of the principle of double effect to help discern the rightness or wrongness of actions that will have both good and evil effects.

Appendix II: The Formation of Conscience. The discussion in Questions 49–55 underscores the need for the suggestions in this appendix. Question 54 introduces the appendix, which offers practical means of forming a moral conscience.

Appendix III: Annotated Resources for Further Study. A brief annotated list of further resources for spiritual and moral formation study.

Appendix IV: Glossary. An alphabetical list of key terms and their definitions for quick reference and help in understanding answers to specific questions.

Appendix V: Model of "Catholic Guidelines for Health-Care Agent Appointed by Medical Power of Attorney". An example of a supplement to the Medical Power of Attorney that provides decision-making guidelines to a health-care agent.

We recommend reading the entire work in sequence, but for those interested in quick references to pressing questions, the following approach may be helpful:

1. Review the Table of Contents. The book is arranged in question-and-answer format, with topics grouped under general subject headings for ease of use.
2. Use the Table of Contents for quick reference. Readers may quickly skim each general topic and select the issues and questions of most immediate interest.

For example, if one has a question about whether it is right or wrong to withhold food or water from a seriously ill patient, a quick examination of the Table of Contents will disclose that guidance may be found in Part II, Questions 15–18. If someone is interested in determining whether he may simply rely on his conscience in making end-of-life decisions, a quick review reveals guidance under Part IV, Questions 49–55.

3. As time allows, read the whole book in the order it is written. Reading the whole book in sequence is not necessary to acquire specific answers to specific questions, but it will help with moral formation and give the reader a fuller understanding of moral decision-making and the teaching of the Catholic Church on end-of-life matters.

4. Read the topics, questions, and answers carefully and reflectively. The book is intended to be accessible to the average Catholic layman. Given the nature of the subjects and the disciplines involved, it is not desirable or even possible to "dumb down" the questions involved in end-of-life decision-making. The intention is to present the material uncomplicatedly and define and explain necessary concepts as simply as reasonably advisable. But in the end, this book deals with issues critical to the welfare of one's soul. Time spent reading and contemplating, perhaps even wrestling with, these subjects will be time well spent.

5. Follow the cross-references, which are included to reduce repetition. Each question is designed to stand on its own. To keep the repetition of concepts and ideas to a minimum, the reader may be directed to other questions to complete or fully explain an answer.

I

WHY THIS BOOK IS IMPORTANT

1. What do "end of life" and "end-of-life decisions" mean?

Since there is no universally identifiable period known as the end of life, the phrase simply refers to the time of the approaching closeness of death. "End-of-life decisions" means those decisions a person likely to die soon or his caregivers are called to make regarding his health-care needs and medical treatment.

2. Why are decisions and acts at the end of life important for Christians?

Because it is essential to finish our lives well and to attain the happiness that awaits us. Saint Paul captured the attitude we should have as we near the end of our lives when he wrote: "I have fought the good fight, I have finished the race, I have kept the faith. From now on there is laid up for me the crown of righteousness, which the Lord, the righteous judge, will award to me on that Day, and not only to me but also to all who have loved his appearing" (2 Tim 4:7–8).

Decisions and acts as we age and deal with illness are critical because men make their way to eternity and God by their free, morally good human choices. They move away from God by their morally wrong choices, but they still must face eternity. Not only are morally bad human choices evil, but they can often be crimes against human nature.[1] Thus, making morally sound decisions is a topic of critical importance.

[1] See Congregation for the Doctrine of the Faith, *Letter "Samaritanus bonus" of the Congregation for the Doctrine of the Faith on the Care of Persons in the Critical and Terminal Phases of Life* (September 22, 2020), especially section V, no. 1.

For most of our lives, we invest countless hours and endless labor and energy in a vocation and the attainment, increase, and preservation of perishable things. We often give intense attention to matters of the slightest long-term consequence while giving little thought to the inevitable end of life.

As Saint Robert Bellarmine notes, however, when nearing the end of life, a man is often "compelled, when unprepared, oppressed by disease, and scarcely possessed of reason, to give an account of those things on which when in health, he had perhaps never once reflected".[2] For this reason—to avoid being compelled to reflect upon death and dying when we are least prepared to make good decisions—we ought to consider the end of life and its related decisions as early as possible.

This subject is important to everyone because choices at the end of life inherently involve life-or-death decisions. But end-of-life decision-making has become a spiritual battlefield for souls and, therefore, has particular relevance for Christians.

The Catholic Church teaches that the goal of life on earth is not to preserve our lives here forever or to avoid suffering. It is to make our way to God through Christ.[3] Unity with Christ, honoring him, praising him, and giving him glory should be the goal of our every action and decision while we are on this earth.[4] End-of-life decisions must conform to this same standard. They either bring us closer to eternity with Christ or take us farther away.

---

[2] Robert Bellarmine, *The Art of Dying Well*, trans. John Dalton (London: Richardson and Son, 1845), http://www.saintsbooks.net/books/St.%20Robert%20Bellarmine%20-%20The%20Art%20of%20Dying%20Well.html.

[3] John Hardon, *Modern Catholic Dictionary* (Garden City, NY: Doubleday, 1980), s.v. "Beatific Vision", 58.

[4] See Col 3:17: "And whatever you do, in word or deed, do everything in the name of the Lord Jesus, giving thanks to God the Father through him."

3. Isn't it needlessly morbid to plan now for decisions that will be made at the end of one's life?

No. Such an idea is a thoroughly modern phenomenon and may arise from an unwise reluctance to accept the fact of one's mortality. The "art of dying", which includes more than making good moral decisions at the end of life (see Q. 103), was of universal concern for at least six hundred years before the twentieth century. It was not considered needlessly morbid to think about and plan for a good death. It was considered an expression of practical wisdom and part of living a good life here and now.[5]

A healthy view of the reality of death from a Christian perspective includes the recognition that considering death need not be morbid. It can even be an occasion for comfort and happiness. The Psalmist writes: "Precious in the sight of the Lord is the death of his saints" (Ps 116:15). The dying words of eighteen-year-old Saint Rose of Viterbo to her parents were "I die with joy, for I desire to be united to my God. Live, so as not to fear death. For those who live well in the world, death is not frightening, but sweet and precious."[6]

While a person should not "keep his mind exclusively on his 'last hour,' on parting and departing",[7] the Catholic Church "encourages us to prepare ourselves for the

---

[5] The *Ars moriendi* (*The Art of Dying: A New Annotated Translation*, trans. Columba Thomas [Philadelphia: The National Catholic Bioethics Center, 2021]) was one of the most popular and influential texts of the late Middle Ages for Catholic laymen and the standard for deathbed religious practice. Bellarmine's *The Art of Dying Well* was written in 1620 and was also immensely popular.

[6] Léon (de Clary), *Lives of the Saints and Blesseds of the Three Orders of Saint Francis* (Taunton, UK: Franciscan Convent, 1886), 107, https://archive.org/stream/livesofsaintsble03leon/livesofsaintsble03leon_djvu.txt.

[7] Josef Pieper, *Death and Immortality* (South Bend, IN: St. Augustine's Press, 2000), 3.

hour of our death".[8] Death is a result of original sin, so in merely natural terms, the thought of it may be frightening. But we were created by God for the supernatural end of eternal life with him, and "our hearts find no peace until they rest in [him]."[9] From this perspective, the approach of death can produce blessings.[10] It can help us to prepare for the everlasting joy that awaits those who place their hope in God.

4. Shouldn't medicine and physicians guide our decision-making in serious illness and approaching death?

Not exclusively. Doctors and other medical providers have a particular and vital role to play in assisting their patients with end-of-life decisions. There are important reasons, however, not to relinquish all decisions at the end of life to medical providers. There is no guarantee that medical providers will be familiar with and well-formed in Catholic moral principles, and in fact, the likelihood is that they will not have such a formation. Moreover, despite the obvious benefits of medicine and medical providers, there is a well-intended tendency toward an entrenched "conveyor belt" mentality in medicine and hospitals today.[11]

---

[8] *Catechism of the Catholic Church*, no. 1014. While the Catholic Church explicitly encourages Catholics to prepare for the time of their death carefully, it is true as well that even for non-Catholics, there is a solemn duty as death approaches to make peace with God according to one's conscience and convictions and the grace at one's disposal.

[9] Augustine, *Confessions*, trans. R. S. Pine-Coffin (New York: Penguin Classics, 1961), 21.

[10] Rev 14:13: "And I heard a voice from heaven saying, 'Write this: Blessed are the dead who from now on die in the Lord.' 'Blessed indeed,' says the Spirit, 'that they may rest from their labors, for their deeds follow them!'"

[11] L. S. Dugdale, *The Lost Art of Dying Well: Reviving Forgotten Wisdom* (New York: HarperCollins, 2020), 12–14.

It is always critical for the patient and his loved ones to weigh the risks and benefits of medical treatment from the perspective of the Church's teachings and in consultation with their medical providers.

Such decisions are governed by moral principles binding upon doctors and patients. As Pope Pius XII noted in an address to participants in the VIII Congress of the World Medical Association: "The absolute character of moral demands remains constant, whether man pays heed to them or not. Moral duty is not dependent upon the pleasure of man! He is only concerned with moral action. The absolute character of the moral order, a phenomenon to which men have always been able to attest, compels us to acknowledge that medical ethics are, in the final analysis, rooted in the transcendental, and subject to higher authority."[12]

While it is true that medical providers play a privileged role in helping us make the right decisions in serious illnesses and at the end of life, they are not our only advisors. We need the assistance of those trained in making moral decisions, well-formed clerics, and most of all, the authoritative guidance of the Church.

5. If this subject is so important, why is there so much conflicting information about dealing with serious illness and dying?

Unfortunately, it can hardly come as a surprise to most Catholics that our culture has become increasingly hostile to the Christian faith and worldview. Ancient truths long held have been directly challenged over the last decades and, in many cases, overthrown and replaced with a secular, materialistic, and relativistic worldview.

[12] Pius XII, Address to Participants in the VIII Congress of the World Medical Association (September 30, 1954), no. 3.

Part of this overthrow and replacement has affected even the meaning of commonly used words and phrases. The following is a non-exhaustive list of words and phrases that are often misused by those inside and outside the medical profession that make clear thinking about the end of life difficult: death with dignity, right to die, quality of life, elimination of all suffering, suffering has no value, and autonomy (see Part IV for a discussion of these concepts and other hindrances to moral decision-making at the end of life).

The constant use of the above concepts and similar ones can obscure the natural law written on the heart and confuse even devout Christians on the teachings of the Bible and the Church.

6. What does morality have to do with medical and practical end-of-life decisions?

First, we must understand what "morals" means, as the term is used in this book. Morals concern right living—the things we do. To have an objective foundation, morals must be based on the moral law (see QQ. 87–92). They are, in fact, deductions, logical conclusions of the teachings of the moral law. Insofar as any person follows the moral law known by reason (see Q. 90), he can make a good moral decision (see Q. 92).

In the fullest sense, however, knowledge of right living comes from the knowledge of God and the revealed moral law (see Q. 91). Right living proceeds from right thinking. Truth or error in the mind tends to result in truth or error in everyday acts and decisions. We know God by faith, which is a firm assent of the mind to revealed truth.[13] We

---

[13] *Summa Theologia* II-II, q. 1, a. 1; q. 2, a. 2. Revealed truth is known through faith when assented to because it is revealed by God and manifested in Sacred Scripture and the teachings of the Church.

serve God by moral living, but according to the Scriptures and the Catholic Church's teaching, a person cannot serve God by moral living without his help.[14] While persons are responsible for making good moral decisions, such decisions—and this book—presuppose that God will help those who earnestly desire to serve him by moral living.

The rapid development of medical advancements, accompanied by the general and universal decline in morality, has given rise to new threats against human life and dignity. The battleground where these new threats are faced is end-of-life decisions. Every day, decisions are made that either imperil souls or move them farther along the path toward ultimate happiness and everlasting life with God.

Since everyone will ultimately age and approach the end of life, and the moral choices we make have consequences now and for eternity, it is imperative to make good decisions in response to the concrete circumstances of aging and death.

7. I am not a scientist. How can I be certain that I have made the right end-of-life decisions?

In making end-of-life decisions, what is required of us is moral certitude, not absolute certainty. Only God possesses absolute certainty of things.[15] Moral certitude is that certainty with which people make judgments about the rational and regular conduct of human beings. It is the firm

---

[14] *Catechism of the Catholic Church*, no. 1999: "The grace of Christ is the gratuitous gift that God makes to us of his own life, infused by the Holy Spirit into our soul to heal it of sin and to sanctify it"; see also Ephesians 2:8–9, 2 Timothy 1:9, Titus 2:11–12.

[15] See John Paul II, Address of the Holy Father John Paul II to the 18th International Congress of the Transplantation Society (August 29, 2000), no. 5: "This moral certainty is considered the necessary and sufficient basis for an ethically correct course of action."

assent of the mind to known truth, excluding any fear of error and motivated by evidence. In the context of end-of-life decisions, it is the firm assent of the mind to the moral rightness of an action or treatment without fear of error.[16] It is certainly short of the absolute certainty that only God possesses, but it is a level of certainty that is enough to inform the action of an ordinarily prudent person.

Scientific knowledge does not increase the certainty that a judgment is true. You can be as certain of the rightness of a moral decision on an end-of-life question as about anything else you know. A particular decision may be complex, but guided by the moral law and the Church's teaching and in consultation with competent medical professionals, you can reach a morally sound decision for yourself or your loved one.

8. Will this book provide all the tools I need to reach moral end-of-life decisions?

It will provide the tools necessary to reach moral decisions, but it will not answer every question you might have. The book is a helpful guide to analyzing and understanding the moral issues that may arise when a tragedy strikes or a loved one falls seriously ill—and understanding them *before* that occurs. It also provides the basic tools necessary to reach sound decisions regarding those issues.

We hope that reading this book will spur the reader, together with other close members of the reader's family, to gain better formation of conscience on end-of-life moral issues by studying closely, pondering deeply, and discussing thoroughly the Church's teachings that inform end-of-life decisions. After reading this book, the reader

[16] See Hardon, *Modern Catholic Dictionary,* s.v. "Certitude" and "Moral Certitude".

is encouraged to examine more deeply the Church's rich two-thousand-year deposit of faith, including an analysis of relevant Scripture, encyclicals, council documents, examples of the saints, and other compendia of moral teaching that touch on this critical area.

While this book does not provide a concrete answer to every possible end-of-life medical scenario, it will help the reader understand the general teachings of the Church and know the right questions to ask about a dying loved one's situation.

II

WHAT THE CHURCH TEACHES ABOUT CARING FOR THE SERIOUSLY ILL AND DYING

9. Where do I start to determine whether a specific medical treatment or intervention is morally required?

A person is required to use only ordinary (also called proportionate) means of medical treatment. The United States Conference of Catholic Bishops describes ordinary means as treatments that "in the judgment of the patient [see Q. 21], offer a reasonable hope of benefit and do not entail an excessive burden or impose excessive expense on the family or the community."[1] The Church often refers to treatments that are disproportionate to the benefit they offer as "disproportionate or extraordinary treatments" (see Q. 19) or "aggressive medical treatments" (see Q. 22). For a discussion of the meaning of "reasonable" in this context, see Q. 27.

The determination of whether a particular medical treatment offers a reasonable hope of benefit and does not entail an excessive burden or expense is made "according to circumstances of persons, places, times, and culture".[2] This means a decision depends on the "concrete circumstances" of that patient.[3] For example, consideration should be given to his age, whether his death is considered

[1] United States Conference of Catholic Bishops, *Ethical and Religious Directives for Catholic Health Care Services* Sixth Edition (Washington, DC: United States Conference of Catholic Bishops, 2018), no. 56.

[2] Pius XII, Address to an International Congress of Anesthesiologists (November 24, 1957), https://liberty4lifeorg.files.wordpress.com/2019/03/pius-xii-address-to-intl-congress-of-anesthesiologists-1957.pdf.

[3] John Paul II, encyclical letter *Evangelium vitae* (The Gospel of Life) (March 25, 1995), no. 65.

imminent and unpreventable, whether he is in severe or intolerable pain, whether the treatment will realistically offer a lasting improvement in his condition or prognosis, the risks and side effects of the treatment, his financial condition, and the financial impact on the patient, family, and larger community.

A patient or loved one should begin the decision-making process by asking whether a proposed medical treatment is beneficial or burdensome to the patient. If a consideration of the concrete circumstances of the patient indicates a proposed treatment will be a greater burden to the patient or his family than it will be beneficial to him, the specific medical treatment is not morally required.

10. Isn't it too lenient or too subjective to follow a beneficial-or-burdensome analysis in making treatment decisions?

No. The Church's guidance on this issue is caringly designed for the spiritual good of all its members. One should remember that whether a specific treatment is beneficial or burdensome is not a determination made by the patient or family based upon what they subjectively believe to be true; it is an objective determination made by reason under the guidance of the moral law (see Q. 87) and the Church's constant teaching.

The Christian faith and the Church's guidance encompass the physical well-being of every person, but there is a higher good to consider—the spiritual good. Pope Pius XII noted that if the Church's teaching regarding end-of-life treatment decisions were too strict, it would be "too burdensome for most men and would render the attainment of the higher, more important good too difficult".[4]

[4] Pius XII, International Congress of Anesthesiologists.

This means that while physical health is important, "life, health, all temporal activities, are in fact subordinated to spiritual ends."[5]

Therefore, what is required of people in determining whether a treatment decision is morally obligatory is a good-faith and objective evaluation of the benefits and burdens of the proposed treatment. (For more on the kind of certainty needed for moral decisions, see Q. 7.)

11. What factors should I consider when trying to establish a patient's concrete circumstances to help determine whether a treatment is ordinary or extraordinary?

This determination is specific to individual patients and will vary from person to person, but there are several factors to consider when establishing the "concrete circumstances" of a patient's condition (that is, "circumstances of persons, places, times, and culture"[6]—see Q. 9).

What is the patient's diagnosis and prognosis?

What is the specific treatment or intervention proposed?

How old is the patient, and how is the proposed treatment related to age?

Is the patient's death imminent and inevitable without the proposed medical treatment (see Q. 14)?

Is the patient experiencing severe or intolerable pain that the proposed treatment can improve (see also QQ. 30–32, 62–65)?

[5] Pius XII, International Congress of Anesthesiologists.
[6] Pius XII, International Congress of Anesthesiologists.

Can the treatment realistically be expected to offer substantial improvement in the patient's condition or prognosis?

What are the risks and side effects of the treatment (see Appendix I)?

What financial resources are available to the patient (see Q. 29)?

What impact will the course of treatment have on the financial stability of the patient or his family (see Q. 66)?

The concrete circumstances are critical to determining whether the proposed treatment or medical intervention is ordinary and proportionate care (Q. 9), or, put another way, whether the proposed medical treatment is extraordinary or disproportionate care (see QQ. 9, 19). Since there is no moral obligation to accept or continue with medical care that is extraordinary or disproportionate, one may in good conscience refuse such care or seek its removal.

Establishing the concrete circumstances of a patient is not complex, but it is a very fact-specific analysis, and it turns on the explicit circumstances of an individual patient, extending even to his financial resources and those of his family. It should also be kept in mind that what is excessive expense to a middle-class worker will necessarily differ from what is excessive expense to a multi-millionaire. There is no moral obligation to go bankrupt or impoverish the family to undergo a medical intervention for the sake of temporarily prolonging life during its terminal stages.

On the other hand, neither a patient nor a loved one should decide *solely* on the basis of the costs to reject or withdraw a reasonable treatment option that could extend one's life (see QQ. 27–29), especially if an extension of life allows one to fulfill moral duties to other family members or friends with minimum burden, financial or otherwise.

12. If an analysis of whether a proposed treatment is beneficial or burdensome concludes that the treatment is not morally required, is a patient or loved one free to do more than is required?

Sometimes. Pope Pius XII remarked that "one is not forbidden to take more than the strictly necessary steps to preserve life and health, as long as he does not fail in some more serious duty."[7] For example, as a person approaches death, it is important that he be able to satisfy his remaining moral and family duties, and especially prepare to meet God.[8] Even if a treatment or intervention is not morally required, a patient or loved one may do more than is necessary, provided the course of treatment does not interfere with his more serious duties.

13. By what process can I determine whether a particular medical treatment may be rejected or withdrawn?

The following is a helpful framework for determining whether a specific medical intervention may be refused or, if already in use, discontinued:

When it has been established that the patient's concrete circumstances indicate his death is both "imminent and inevitable" (see Q. 14), ask whether the specific treatment under consideration is "disproportionate or extraordinary" to the prospects for improvement (Q. 19). If the answer is

---

[7] Pius XII, International Congress of Anesthesiologists.
[8] John Paul II, *Evangelium vitae*, no. 65.

"yes", then the specific medical treatment being considered is morally optional.[9]

If, however, the treatment is "proportionate or ordinary" (see Q. 9), it is fundamentally beneficial and thus morally obligatory.[10] Care should be taken to determine whether the means of treatment being proposed or considered is "objectively proportionate to the prospects for improvement".[11]

14. What does it mean when the doctors say that my loved one's death is "imminent and inevitable"?

In matters related to end-of-life decisions, a requirement often arises that death must be "imminent and inevitable". In straightforward terms, to say that death is imminent means that it has been determined that it will happen very soon. To say that death is inevitable means that it has been determined that death cannot be prevented.

Practically speaking, in the context of end-of-life decisions, imminent death is a death that is rapidly approaching—hours or days away. An inevitable death is one that no medical intervention can prevent from happening. These terms are not synonymous: death may be inevitable but not imminent.

[9] United States Conference of Catholic Bishops, *Ethical and Religious Directives for Catholic Health Care Services*, no. 57: "A person may forgo extraordinary or disproportionate means of preserving life"; see also John Paul II, *Evangelium vitae*, no. 65: "When death is clearly imminent and inevitable, one can in conscience 'refuse forms of treatment that would only secure a precarious and burdensome prolongation of life, so long as the normal care to the sick person in similar cases is not interrupted'" (quoting Congregation for the Doctrine of the Faith, *Declaration on Euthanasia* [May 5, 1980], section II).

[10] United States Conference of Catholic Bishops, *Ethical and Religious Directives for Catholic Health Care Services*, no. 56: "A person has a moral obligation to use ordinary or proportionate means of preserving his or her life."

[11] John Paul II, *Evangelium vitae*, no. 65.

15. What is the normal or basic care required for every person who is seriously ill or dying?

The terms usually used to describe the care required for every person are "basic care" or "ordinary care", which refer to nonmedical care such as food, water, blankets, and bathing. It is common sense that food and water are necessities of life, without which anyone would die. Thus, providing nutrition (food) and hydration (water) is basic care for humans, as much for the medically vulnerable as for anyone else.

In 2020, addressing this issue, the Congregation for the Doctrine of the Faith declared that "required basic care for each person includes the administration of the nourishment and fluids."[12] The Congregation further stated that when food and water no longer benefit the patient because the body cannot absorb them or cannot process them, the provision of food and water should be suspended.[13]

16. Isn't providing food and water "medical treatment" rather than basic care?

No. Providing food and water is no more "medical" treatment than providing blankets to a medically vulnerable person. Medical care is precisely that—medical.

By contrast, no reasonable person would deny that feeding and hydrating are basic nonmedical functions necessary to continued human existence. Consequently, with a few exceptions (see Q. 15), a person is always to be provided food and water. This typically includes the artificial provision of food and water (see Q. 18). While this book does not provide legal advice, the laws and definitions of your

---

[12] Congregation for the Doctrine of the Faith, Letter "Samaritanus bonus" of the Congregation for the Doctrine of the Faith on the Care of Persons in the Critical and Terminal Phases of Life (September 22, 2020), section III.

[13] Congregation for the Doctrine of the Faith, Samaritanus bonus, section III.

state should be carefully reviewed because some statutes erroneously consider food and water to be a form of medical treatment (for such legal considerations see QQ. 107–18).[14]

In addition to basic care (food and water), a patient, regardless of his medical condition or prognosis, is always to be provided "comfort" care—that is, basic care such as bathing, grooming, clean clothes, and rotation of his body to prevent bed sores. Together, basic and comfort care are the minimum owed to any human being in any setting, subject only to a few exceptions.

The teaching of the Catholic Church is clear that food and water "do not constitute medical therapy in a proper sense.... They are instead forms of obligatory care of the patient, representing both a primary clinical and unavoidable human response to the sick person."[15]

17. If providing food and water isn't medical care, why did my loved one's doctor tell the family it is?

Common among physicians and in the literature of the medical profession today is the assertion that basic care (see Q. 15) is "medical therapy" or "medical treatment" rather than ordinary care due to human beings at all stages of life.

The argument is that while physicians are obligated to provide basic care (because not to do so would cause harm), they are not obligated to provide medical treatments they believe are ineffective to patients. The deadly reality of such

---

[14] See, e.g., Texas Health and Safety Code, Title 2, Subtitle H, Chapter 166, "Advance Directives Act", §166.002 (10), which defines the artificial administration of nutrition and hydration as "life-sustaining treatment" rather than basic care: " 'Life-sustaining treatment' means treatment that, based on reasonable medical judgment, sustains the life of a patient and without which the patient will die. The term includes both life-sustaining medications ... and artificially administered nutrition and hydration."

[15] Congregation for the Doctrine of the Faith, *Samaritanus bonus*, section III.

a redefinition is that it is used as an attempted justification of the individual actions of physicians and the work of legislatures to withhold or deny food and water through a feeding tube to patients who are not actively dying (as was done, for example, in the well-known case of Terri Schiavo[16]).

This misrepresentation of basic care as medical treatment calls into question the motives and presuppositions of those who engage in it. Reasonable persons do not ordinarily argue that food and water are not essential to sustaining human life. The fact that a patient must receive food and water through a feeding tube because of illness or injury does not transform the provision of that food and water from basic care into medical care. The same applies to bathing, grooming, or rotating the patient's body to prevent bed sores. The fact that a medical technician provides these services does not convert them into medical care.

18. Does basic care include the provision of food and water by artificial means?

Yes. The artificial provision (by feeding tube) of food and water to the seriously ill and dying incapable of taking them

[16] In 1990, at the age of twenty-six, Terri Schiavo, an otherwise healthy young woman, suffered a sudden cardiac arrest. The cause remains a mystery, but Terri was subsequently diagnosed with neurological injury caused by a lack of oxygen to the brain. She was placed on a ventilator but could soon breathe on her own. Several doctors diagnosed Terri as being in a persistent vegetative state, but she was neither comatose nor "brain dead". She was not in the process of dying, nor was she terminally ill. Her heart beat on its own, and she did not require any assistance to breathe. She could not, however, feed herself without help. She was thus provided food and water by artificial means (through a feeding tube). Terri's husband argued that his wife would never have wanted to live in such a condition and attempted to have the feeding tube removed. Her parents disagreed and sought to keep her alive. The matter ended up in the courts, where it languished for years. Eventually, Terri's husband prevailed, and after more than thirteen days without food or water, Terri died on March 31, 2005.

orally is required, "provided that it does not cause harm or intolerable suffering to the patient".[17] This is consistent with the beneficial or burdensome analysis above (Q. 9).

The *Ethical and Religious Directives for Catholic Health Care Services* promulgated by the United States Conference of Catholic Bishops makes it clear that "This obligation [providing food and water] extends to patients in chronic and presumably irreversible conditions (e.g., the 'persistent vegetative state') who can reasonably be expected to live indefinitely if given such care."[18] This obligation to provide medically assisted food and water (by feeding tube) becomes morally optional, however, when it can no longer reasonably be expected to prolong life or when it would cause significant physical discomfort or be excessively burdensome for the patient.[19]

19. What are disproportionate or extraordinary treatments?

Given that all men are created in the image of God and thus possess inherent dignity, all people have a duty to care for their health. Those whose task is to care for the sick must "administer the remedies [to an ailing body] that seem necessary or useful".[20]

No one is required, however, to take advantage of all possible remedies (treatments) that might exist, but only

[17] Congregation for the Doctrine of the Faith, *Samaritanus bonus*, section III.

[18] United States Conference of Catholic Bishops, *Ethical and Religious Directives for Catholic Health Care Services*, no. 59. See also John Paul II, Life-Sustaining Treatments and Vegetative State (March 20, 2004), no. 4, where he says that the provision of food and water, even by artificial means, "always represents a *natural means* of preserving life, not a *medical act*" (emphasis in original).

[19] United States Conference of Catholic Bishops, *Ethical and Religious Directives for Catholic Health Care Services*, no. 58.

[20] Congregation for the Doctrine of the Faith, *Declaration on Euthanasia*, section IV.

the remedies that offer a reasonable hope of benefit to the patient[21] (see Q. 9 for an introduction to the terms "disproportionate" and "extraordinary").

Simply stated, extraordinary medical treatments are those that do not offer a reasonable hope of benefit to a patient.[22] A patient is not obliged to attempt remedies through such means, because the help they can reasonably expect to offer the patient is disproportionate to the end they may bring about. For example, a person is not obligated to use a particular experimental treatment that will significantly increase his pain or impose an excessive expense on his family when the reasonably expected end is that his life might be prolonged for a brief period.

20. Isn't the rejection or removal of disproportionate or extraordinary treatments the same as killing oneself or a loved one?

No. Acceptance of the inevitability of death by natural causes, by declining disproportionate medical interventions, is clearly distinguished from suicide and euthanasia. In the former, what takes the patient's life is the underlying disease, *not* the refusal or removal of the medical treatment. The mere *foreknowledge* that death will occur is not the same as *the intent to bring about* death. By contrast, suicide and euthanasia are intended to kill the patient.

The well-reasoned and prayerful decision by a patient to forgo extraordinary treatments is an acknowledgment

---

[21] Congregation for the Doctrine of the Faith, *Declaration on Euthanasia*, section IV.

[22] See United States Conference of Catholic Bishops, *Ethical and Religious Directives for Catholic Health Care Services*, no. 57: "A person may forgo extraordinary or disproportionate means of preserving life. Disproportionate means are those that in the patient's judgment do not offer a reasonable hope of benefit or entail an excessive burden, or impose excessive expense on the family or the community."

that he has reached the culmination of his life. By all appearances, the harm of further medical interventions outweighs the possible benefit. "To forgo extraordinary or disproportionate means is not the equivalent of suicide or euthanasia; it rather expresses acceptance of the human condition in the face of death."[23]

When a military leader in a just war gives a necessary command to his forces to attack a heavily fortified enemy position to liberate innocent captives, he can reasonably foresee that many of his soldiers will die. He does not, however, by giving the assault order, become a mass murderer of his troops. His intent is not to kill his soldiers but to liberate innocent captives.[24] The fact that he could reasonably foresee those deaths does not convert his noble intention (liberation) into an evil one (willing the death of his men). For further discussion of the distinction between foreseeing and intending, see Appendix I.

Similarly, when a proper moral decision is made to forgo or discontinue an extraordinary or disproportionate medical intervention, the fact that one can reasonably foresee that such an action will lead to the death of the patient does not mean that death is intended. Simply put, the underlying disease takes the patient's life, and the intent to forgo extraordinary medical interventions is to accept the reality of death when the proposed treatment offers no reasonable hope of benefit or is excessively burdensome.

21. Isn't "in the patient's judgment" just another way of saying a patient can base a decision on his own subjective opinion?

[23] John Paul II, *Evangelium vitae*, 65.

[24] This example is from Judge Andrew Kleinfeld's dissenting opinion in *Compassion in Dying v. Washington*, 79 F.3d 790, 858 (9th Circuit Court of Appeals 1996).

No. The United States Conference of Catholic Bishops uses this phrase in Ethical and Religious Directive no. 57 (see footnote 21 above). Still, such usage is not intended to ground moral decision-making in one's subjective opinions. The Church respects the patient's judgment (as noted in Q. 9), but "in the patient's judgment" refers to a patient who is mentally capable of making medical and health-care decisions and free from coercion. Crucially, it presupposes that this judgment is morally sound (that is, consistent with the Church's teaching). As Ethical and Religious Directive no. 59 more fully explains: "The free and informed judgment made by a competent adult patient concerning the use or withdrawal of life-sustaining procedures should always be respected and normally complied with, *unless* it is contrary to Catholic moral teaching."[25]

The "judgment of the patient" in this context presumes that the person's decision in a given case is based on the guiding moral principles already in that person's well-formed conscience (see QQ. 49–55).

22. I have been told I can decline aggressive medical treatments. What does that mean?

The term "aggressive medical treatments" is widely used but has no generally accepted definition. In medical literature, the term is often undefined or appears as a catchphrase for a list of life-sustaining medical interventions including, but not limited to, artificial nutrition or hydration, invasive ventilation, cardiopulmonary resuscitation, or blood transfusion.[26] For the more useful and specific criterion of

---

[25] United States Conference of Catholic Bishops, *Ethical and Religious Directives for Catholic Health Care Services*, no. 59 (emphasis added).

[26] See, e.g., Ying Hsin Hsu et al., "The Trend of Aggressive Treatments in End-of-Life Care for Older People with Dementia after a Policy Change in Taiwan", *The Journal of Post-Acute and Long-Term Care Medicine* 21, no. 6 (June 1, 2020).

"disproportionate and extraordinary means" used in this book, see QQ. 9 and 19.

23. I have a loved one with a severe brain injury, and his doctors say he is in a "persistent vegetative state". What does that mean?

The term "persistent vegetative state" was first used in 1972.[27] The word "vegetative" was a poor choice from the beginning, but the term is now solidly established in medical usage.[28] As commonly used today, the "vegetative state" is a condition of deep unconsciousness in which there is complete unawareness of the self and the environment.[29] Patients diagnosed as being in a *persistent* vegetative state are those who are not expected to recover consciousness and who have been in a vegetative state for at least a month after the event that led to the initial diagnosis.[30]

Patients in this condition may open their eyes, follow movement with them, or be startled by loud or sudden noises. Although it is considered unlikely that they will recover, they are not in imminent danger of death and may live indefinitely, provided they receive food and water through artificial means (feeding tubes). For this reason, it

[27] Bryan Jennett and Fred Plum, "Persistent Vegetative State after Brain Damage: A Syndrome in Search of a Name", *The Lancet* 299, no. 7753 (April 1, 1972).

[28] No human being, no matter how disabled, should be considered a "vegetable". From conception, human beings are ordered to God and endowed with a spiritual soul and with intellect and free will. Even in the severest circumstances in which a person's capacity for exercising the mind and free will is diminished, he remains a human being with a spiritual soul ordered toward God.

[29] The Multi-Society Task Force on PVS, "Medical Aspects of the Persistent Vegetative State, Pt. 1", *New England Journal of Medicine* 330, no. 21 (1994).

[30] The Multi-Society Task Force on PVS, "Medical Aspects of the Persistent Vegetative State".

is doubtful whether the condition of a persistent vegetative state is an end-of-life issue.[31]

24. Is it possible to recover from a persistent vegetative state?

Yes. As Pope John Paul II noted in his 2004 address to the International Congress on Life-Sustaining Treatments and Vegetative State: Scientific Advances and Ethical Dilemmas, "We must neither forget nor underestimate that there are well-documented cases of at least partial recovery even after many years [from a persistent vegetative state]; we can thus state that medical science, up until now, is still unable to predict with certainty who among patients in this condition will recover and who will not."[32]

Precisely because there are well-documented cases of at least partial recovery from a persistent vegetative state, there are those in medical, ethical, and legal professions who believe the diagnosis itself is problematic, and even that "it is one of the most arbitrary and subjectively applied diagnoses in clinical practice."[33]

[31] The persistent vegetative state is addressed in this book only because it is generally included in any discussion of end-of-life decision-making. Also, it is often a medical diagnosis of persistent vegetative state that serves as the basis for a recommendation to cease specific medical treatments and even basic life-sustaining care in some instances. For reasons mentioned above, illustrated by examples in answer to Q. 25, we do not believe "persistent vegetative state" is rightly considered an end-of-life issue, and this should be made clear in any Catholic teaching on serious illness and the end of life. To merely parrot current medical usage and understanding without explanation may lead to further confusion among Catholics, making moral decision-making more complicated than necessary.

[32] John Paul II, "Life-Sustaining Treatments and Vegetative State". He calls the persistent vegetative state "only a conventional prognostic judgment, relative to the fact that the recovery of patients, statistically speaking, is ever more difficult as the condition of vegetative state is prolonged in time."

[33] Bobby Schindler, "Basic Care, Human Dignity, and Care for Medically Vulnerable Persons", On Point 18 (November 2017).

25. What are some documented examples of those who have recovered after a diagnosis of a persistent vegetative state?

A fascinating study of a particular drug therapy in one hospital concludes that the prognosis for recovery of adult patients in a vegetative state after traumatic brain injury remains poor but reports three cases of interest.[34]

A fourteen-year-old boy suffered a traumatic brain injury from a traffic accident. He was comatose upon arrival at the hospital, and three months after the trauma, he was able to breathe through a tracheostomy. He sometimes seemed awake, although his eyes could not follow moving objects, and he could not obey simple verbal commands. He was diagnosed as being in a persistent vegetative state and provided nutrition, hydration, and drug therapy through a gastric tube. One year after the trauma, the young man could walk to high school alone.

A second case involved a twenty-seven-year-old man who experienced a severe head injury from a traffic accident and was comatose upon arrival at the hospital. He had a tracheostomy tube and a gastric tube inserted, and he sometimes seemed awake, although his eyes could not follow moving objects and he could not obey simple verbal commands. He was diagnosed as being in a persistent vegetative state, and there was no improvement one year after the trauma. Drug therapy was administered through

[34] See W. Matsuda et al., "Awakenings from Persistent Vegetative State: Report of Three Cases with Parkinsonism and Brain Stem Lesions on MRI", *Journal of Neurology, Neurosurgery & Psychiatry* 74, no. 11 (November 2003). This article does not advocate views advanced in this book or generally address persistent vegetative state. It references the three case studies cited to illustrate the possibility of treating some patients in a persistent vegetative state who would otherwise remain bedridden for the rest of their lives with the particular drug noted in the study.

the gastric tube. Ten months after beginning treatment, he began to use a word processor to express his thoughts. After a year, he was extubated. He said, "I want to eat sushi and drink beer."

A third case involved a fifty-one-year-old man who was comatose with a traumatic brain injury after a traffic accident. He had a tracheostomy and a gastric tube, and he could not obey simple verbal commands and was diagnosed as being in a persistent vegetative state. Seven months after his injury, drug therapy was begun through the gastric tube. Two months later, he was extubated and could say his name and address correctly. Six months after beginning treatment, he was transferred to another hospital to continue rehabilitation.

26. I have a terminally ill family member who has been told that a particular treatment will only result in a "burdensome prolongation of life". What does that mean?

"Burdensome prolongation of life" is another phrase sometimes used in the determination of whether a specific treatment is beneficial or burdensome (see Q. 9). As it is commonly used, the phrase refers to the results of a treatment that provides a minimal extension of life by unreasonably "aggressive medical interventions" that "no longer correspond to the real situation of the patient".[35] The phrase is used to describe medical procedures used to prolong life that offer no cure, no reasonable hope for the patient to return to the life he lived before the onset of his disease, and no substantial improvement in his condition or prognosis.

[35] See John Paul II, *Evangelium vitae*, no. 65.

It is important to note that the term is not a value judgment. It does not mean that the patient's circumstances make his life no longer valuable so that he is a burden to society. The term, adequately understood, is intended to help analyze a treatment or intervention according to the benefit it can provide to the patient to determine whether the patient's benefit is disproportionate to specific medical interventions or treatments (for more on proportionality between treatment and benefit, see Q. 9).

27. What is a "reasonable hope of benefit"?

There is no generally accepted definition for "reasonable hope of benefit". Unfortunately, the meaning of the phrase is commonly presumed. The term is ordinarily used as if self-evident in formulating an understanding of disproportionate or extraordinary treatments (see Q. 19). For a benefit to be reasonable, it must, at the very least, not be irrational and must be grounded in medical reality, including the diagnosis of the patient, the specific prognosis, and the availability, success rates, cost, and burdens of any helpful medical interventions and drug regimens and therapies. Uninformed, unfounded, or subjective desires for benefits untethered from relevant medical facts are unreasonable. Of course, in all cases, no medical treatment may be considered reasonable if it violates the moral law (see Q. 83).

28. What does "excessive expense" mean?

The term "excessive expense" is frequently used in documents related to end-of-life care. The Church uses the term to determine whether a specific treatment is beneficial or burdensome (see Q. 26). While we must care for ourselves, we do not have an obligation to do so at all costs. Duty does not usually require the destitution of oneself or one's family. Economic considerations must never, however, be the *sole criterion* for any end-of-life decision.

Questions that may be considered in determining excessive expense include the out-of-pocket cost for any particular intervention, assistance from insurance, what, if any, benefit is being derived for the sums expended, and the long-term economic impact on one's family in proportion to the benefit received by the patient.

There is a significant difference between paying a large amount for open-heart surgery that repairs a defective heart valve, extending a fifty-year-old patient's life by decades, and incurring high costs for similar interventions for a person much closer to death. The key is to avoid the extremes of either choosing not to accept costly medical interventions based on cost-efficiency alone or demanding costly interventions despite the lack of reasonable expectation of any concrete health benefits.

29. If economic cost may not be the *sole* criterion in end-of-life decisions, does that mean a consideration of the cost of medical treatment or intervention has no place in end-of-life decision-making?

Caution is always in order when discussing the economic impact of end-of-life treatments on patients and families because it is a symptom of the modern "culture of death" to see "the growing number of elderly and disabled people as intolerable and too burdensome".[36] As Pope John Paul II points out, "In this context the temptation grows to have recourse to euthanasia, that is, to take control of death and bring it about before its time, 'gently' ending

[36] John Paul II, *Evangelium vitae*, no. 64.

one's own life or the life of others."[37] Thus, those making end-of-life decisions are vulnerable to manipulation over concerns about economic costs and burdens to the family. Nonetheless, the economic impact of medical treatments is one important criterion in moral end-of-life decisions.

In simple terms, a moral balance must always be maintained between not bankrupting one's family by embracing treatments that offer no reasonable hope of benefit and not being manipulated to believe that one's life is intolerable, no longer of value, or too burdensome to family or society. This balance must be negotiated with prayer, reason, and guileless consultation with medical professionals, family, and spiritual advisors (see QQ. 26–28 for further guidance).

30. When death is imminent, is it wrong to relieve suffering with painkillers and sedatives, even when the result is decreased consciousness and a shortening of life?

The heroic endurance of pain without medication is not the duty of all Catholics. Pope Pius XII, in answer to a question presented by a group of physicians, pronounced that it is not wrong to relieve pain by narcotics, even when the result is decreased consciousness and a shortening of life, if no other means of reducing pain exist, and if, in the given circumstances, the treatment does not prevent the carrying out of other religious and moral duties.[38]

[37] John Paul II, *Evangelium vitae*, no. 64.

[38] See John J. Lynch, S.J., "Pain and Anesthesia: A Papal Allocution", *Linacre Quarterly* 24, no. 4 (November 24, 1957), https://epublications.marquette.edu/lnq/vol24/iss4/3. The official text of Pope Pius XII's address, delivered in French, is contained in *Acta Apostolicae Sedis* 49 (March 27, 1957). The English text forming the basis of Lynch's commentary was taken from *The Pope Speaks* 4 (Summer 1957). Lynch does a thorough job of covering the questions and answers addressed by Pope Pius XII. See also Congregation for the Doctrine of the Faith, *Declaration on Euthanasia* (the CDF quotes Pope Pius XII).

Pope Pius XII thus identified three necessary considerations: (1) whether other means of relieving pain exist, (2) the given circumstances of the patient's condition, and (3) whether the patient's moral and religious duties to prepare himself to meet God would be obstructed. Such religious duties include confessing sins with true contrition, worthy reception of the Eucharist (if the condition of the patient permits), and a final expression of love for one's spouse and children.[39]

In his encyclical *Evangelium vitae* Pope John Paul II confirmed Pope Pius XII's statement. He wrote:

> In such a case, death is not willed or sought, even though for reasonable motives one runs the risk of it: there is simply a desire to ease pain effectively by using the analgesics which medicine provides. All the same, "it is not right to deprive the dying person of consciousness without a serious reason": as they approach death people ought to be able to satisfy their moral and family duties, and above all they ought to be able to prepare in a fully conscious way for their definitive meeting with God.[40]

31. What role does intention play in the use of pain medications and sedatives?

Key to the moral use of pain medicine in end-of-life decisions is the role *intention* plays (see discussion in Q. 100). A patient may receive, and a health-care professional may administer, a medication that could hasten death or render the patient unconscious if the *sole intent* in administering the pain-relieving drug is to prevent pain, and *not* to

[39] See John Paul II, *Evangelium vitae*, no. 65 (quoting Pope Pius XII's Address to an International Group of Physicians [February 24, 1957], section III, *Acta Apostolicae Sedis* 49 [March 27, 1957], 145).

[40] John Paul II, *Evangelium vitae*, no. 65 (quoting Pope Pius XII's Address to an International Group of Physicians, 145).

hasten the patient's death. The intention is critical. The use of pain medications when death is imminent must not be a back door to assisted suicide or euthanasia.

Suppose one's intent is pure in administering or receiving painkillers and sedatives (that is, there is no direct intention to kill the patient). In that case, the fact that one can reasonably foresee a possible but unintended harmful effect does not render the act of providing or using certain drugs immoral. The moral principle in play is called the "principle of double effect" (see Appendix I).

32. What is palliative care? Is it possible to eliminate all suffering through palliative care medicine or other appropriate means?

Palliative care is specialized medical care that provides relief from symptoms resulting from serious illness. In contrast to curative care (which is meant to cure a disease), palliative care is meant to make the patient more comfortable. It is administered by a team of doctors, nurses, and others with special training and complements the other care (including curative care) a patient may be receiving. It is intended to augment a person's ongoing care by improving his quality of life as much as possible. Palliative care can help reduce pain and suffering, but it is not possible to eliminate it altogether. For a discussion on the Christian understanding of the meaning of suffering, see QQ. 61–65.

33. What is hospice care, and are all hospice care facilities appropriate for Catholics?

No, not all hospice care is appropriate for Catholics. Hospice care is comfort care that addresses disease symptoms when no cure is possible, and it can be a great blessing during the last six months of a patient's life. We recommend that only hospice facilities that operate consistently with the end-of-life teachings of the Catholic Church be considered.

Determining whether a particular hospice does or does not follow the Church's teachings is not always an easy task, but it is critical. We suggest contacting local diocesan offices for recommendations of excellent hospice facilities operating in the area. Speaking with families with hospice experience for their dying loved ones and medical professionals familiar with Catholic moral teachings is also very helpful.

III

THE CHURCH'S TEACHING
ON DEATH AND SPECIFIC
END-OF-LIFE DECISIONS

34. What is "death"?

Since this book deals with more than medical issues, it is helpful to approach the question of death and its determination broadly. In brief, death is the cessation of the bodily functions of a human being. Perhaps the best explanation for how this occurs is a theological explanation: the cessation of bodily functions occurs when the soul departs the body, for the human person is a unity of body and soul, which form one human nature.

Theologically, then, human death is "the separation of the soul from the body".[1] It "is the end of man's earthly pilgrimage, of the time of grace and mercy which God offers him so as to work out his earthly life in keeping with the divine plan, and to decide his ultimate destiny".[2]

Death is a consequence of Adam's sin, as stated by Saint Paul: "Therefore as sin came into the world through one man and death through sin, and so death spread to all men because all men sinned" (Rom 5:12). Death is thus natural only with regard to matter (the corruptible body) and not the soul (the incorruptible form of the body).[3]

As the *Catechism* tells us, "The Church encourages us to prepare ourselves for the hour of our death."[4] In the Church's ancient Litany of the Saints, we pray: "From a sudden and unforeseen death, deliver us, O Lord",[5] and we ask the Blessed Virgin Mary to intercede for us "at the hour of our death".

---

[1] *Catechism of the Catholic Church*, no. 997.
[2] *Catechism of the Catholic Church*, no. 997.
[3] Thomas Aquinas, *Summa Theologiae* I-II, q. 85, a. 6.
[4] *Catechism of the Catholic Church*, no. 1014.
[5] *Roman Missal*, Litany of the Saints.

35. The term "body" seems straightforward, but what is meant by the term "soul"?

The human person is a unity of body and soul. The human body is mortal and physical, and the soul is the immortal spiritual principle in man that animates his body.[6] The soul is individually created for each person by God. This is why human life must be protected from conception to natural death. We are created in the image of God and endowed by God with a spiritual soul at the moment of conception.[7]

When we say that the soul "animates" the body, we mean that the soul is the life-giving principle of the body. This understanding is why we call living things "animate" and nonliving things "inanimate".[8] Animals are living things that possess a mortal (perishable) animal soul, and plants are living things that have a mortal (perishable) plant soul. Man possesses a rational and spiritual soul that cannot die. He has a soul different from that of other living things because his end differs from that of every other living thing. His end is supernatural life with God. It is impossible, therefore, rationally to maintain that death is the final destiny of man. Such a position reduces man to merely the physical, material order.

The fact that man has a spiritual soul means that it is ordered to a supernatural end, and his soul can achieve communion with God.[9] These aspects of a human being— body and soul—are inseparable in life and make up one human nature. The soul is temporarily separated from the body at death (see Q. 34) "but will be reunited with the body at the final resurrection."[10]

[6] See *Catechism of the Catholic Church*, nos. 362–67.

[7] John Hardon, *Modern Catholic Dictionary* (Garden City, NY: Doubleday, 1980), s.v. "Soul", 514.

[8] Thomas Aquinas, *Summa Theologiae*, I, q. 75, a. 1.

[9] See *Catechism of the Catholic Church*, no. 367.

[10] *Catechism of the Catholic Church*, no. 366.

36. How do we know when death occurs?

At first glance, this might seem like a silly question. In the past, people could determine death when bodily functions ceased and the process of decay began. But in this modern age, advancements in medicine have made it more difficult than one might assume to determine the precise moment death occurs—for current medical technology allows life to be prolonged more than previously imaginable. This is further complicated by the fact that the psychology of modern medicine tends to view man as nothing more than a material being.[11] Consequently, serious ethical and moral questions frequently arise.

While it is theologically clear *what* death is, the difficulty lies in knowing *when it occurs*. Simply put, it is impossible to observe the soul separating from the body. Pope John Paul II acknowledged this in an address to the Eighteenth International Congress of the Transplantation Society when he noted that death "is an event *which no scientific technique or empirical method can identify directly*".[12]

In some cases, advancements in medical technology and medical interventions have made ascertaining the fact of death even more difficult. In the context of organ donation, Pope John Paul II mentions, "this gives rise to one of the most debated issues in contemporary bioethics, as well

---

[11] See Introduction, footnote 3, referencing modern psychology's move away from a conception that man is a unity of body and soul to the notion that man is purely material, no different from an animal.

[12] John Paul II, Address of the Holy Father John Paul II to the 18th International Congress of the Transplantation Society (August 29, 2000), no. 4, (emphasis in original). This is why the Catholic Church is, and must always be, very deliberate and measured when discussing technical medical conclusions as to *when* death occurs. In the final analysis, it is not a determination of faith or morals. Therefore, Pope John Paul II speaks in measured terms regarding "brain death": "the *complete* and *irreversible* cessation of all brain activity, if rigorously applied, does not seem to conflict with the essential elements of a sound anthropology" (emphasis in original).

as to serious concerns in the minds of ordinary people. I refer to the problem of *ascertaining the fact of death*. When can a person be considered dead with complete certainty?"[13] (see also Q. 123).

37. Why is knowing the time of death important?

In this time of moral decline combined with extraordinary medical and scientific advancements, immoral decisions with severe consequences for the ill and dying are being made when there is no certainty of death. For example, it is possible that vital organs are being harvested from individuals who are still living.[14]

Pope John Paul II's statement of fact should be taken as a cautionary note. Despite assertions to the contrary, scientific techniques and empirical methods cannot directly identify when the theological reality of death occurs. Thus, every end-of-life decision a Catholic is required to make must be made with this in mind. Science and medicine can only go so far, and it is often not as far as modern practitioners assert.

38. What are the criteria of modern medicine for determining *when* death occurs?

Historically, the most common medical method for determining death has been the use of cardiopulmonary criteria.

---

[13] John Paul II, Transplantation Society, no. 5 (emphasis in original).

[14] This refers, in this context, to the harvesting of organs from living patients who may have donated their organs for use after death, only to have them taken before their actual death. This does not address the current and highly controversial proposal to allow terminally ill patients to donate their organs while alive (called "living donation"). While the Catholic Church has not yet specifically addressed this issue, for this book, it is enough to note that the Church prohibits the disabling mutilation of a person or the premature bringing about of his death even if it helps another person live longer. See *Catechism of the Catholic Church*, no. 2296.

Typically, a physician declared a person dead when the person entirely and irreversibly stopped breathing and his heart stopped beating. Medically, when the heart stopped beating and breathing ceased, blood could no longer be pumped through the body to keep the organs functioning, and they eventually atrophied and died, as did the oxygen-starved brain. This standard is long-established and recognized as noncontroversial.

Advancements in modern medicine, however, have made it increasingly possible to keep a person's heart beating even if traumatic injuries have caused irreversible brain damage. This has led to the view among medical providers that people who have suffered such brain injuries should also be able to be declared dead, even if the cardiopulmonary criteria for death are not present. This view originated from the existence of medical interventions that could keep the heart beating by artificial means (e.g., ventilators).

In 1981, the Uniform Declaration of Death Act (UDDA) was drafted by a President's Commission study on "brain death". The act was intended to provide a model for states to emulate. The UDDA offers two definitions for when an individual may legally be declared dead: irreversible cessation of circulatory and respiratory functions (cardiopulmonary criteria); or irreversible cessation of all functions of the entire brain, including the brain stem (neurological criteria).

39. Most of what I hear these days is about "brain death". What does that mean?

With modern life-support medical technology, such as ventilators, which keeps oxygen flowing throughout the body by pushing air into the lungs, people whose breathing and heartbeats would otherwise have ceased can now be kept artificially (that is, mechanically) alive. Undoubtedly, this intervention has led many seriously ill and compromised patients to make astonishing recoveries. It has also led to patients with complete and irreversible brain damage entering a state of "irreversible and apnoeic coma", which came to be known colloquially as "brain death".[15]

Because people whose heartbeat and breathing had ceased have afterward recovered, tests were developed to determine whether true death of the brain, from which no one has been revived, had occurred.[16] A diagnosis of brain death has thus increasingly become the medical means of determining death (see Q. 38).

Brain death (also called determination by "neurological criteria") is defined as the complete and irreversible loss of all upper brain function and lower brain stem function. "A person determined to be brain dead is legally and clinically dead."[17] This determination of brain death "is primarily clinical"[18] and requires essential findings that can, in some cases, be certified by a single physician.

40. What are some of the problems associated with using brain death as a criterion for death?

Determination of death by neurological criteria (brain death) is hotly contested in the medical profession and the Church. Also, as John Haas writes, "It must be admitted

[15] Matthew Hanley, *Determining Death by Neurological Criteria: Current Practice and Ethics* (Philadelphia: The National Bioethics Center, Washington, DC: Catholic University of America Press, 2020), 5.

[16] John M. Haas, "Catholic Teaching Regarding the Legitimacy of Neurological Criteria for the Determination of Death" (2011 Saint John Paul II Lecture Series in Bioethics), https://liberty4life.org/lecture-bioethics-john-haas-neurological-criteria-brain-death/.

[17] Ajay Kumar Goila and Mridula Pawar, "The Diagnosis of Brain Death", *Indian Journal of Critical Care Medicine* 13, no. 1 (January–March 2009), https://www.ncbi.nlm.nih.gov/pmc/articles/PMC2772257/?report=classic#sec1-6title.

[18] Goila and Pawar, "The Diagnosis of Brain Death".

that some physicians will not always be careful in the administration of these tests and may prematurely declare a person to be dead without properly ensuring that the criteria have been met."[19] Regarding diagnostic error in determining brain death, Matthew Hanley also notes that "in addition to claims of systematic abuse, there are reliable accounts of serious errors in making the determination of death."[20] A further concern regarding the use of neurological criteria has arisen in the context of organ donation. Some moral theologians and medical ethicists and a considerable number of lay Catholics have raised serious concerns.[21] In addition, a widespread modern decline in morality, inconsistent application of neurological standards, reliable reports of serious diagnostic errors, and the growing movement to harvest vital organs before death should urge caution.

41. Is there an official Catholic Church teaching on brain death that establishes when death occurs?

No, the Church's magisterial pronouncements to date have not been definitive.[22] At the same time, the Church has carefully evaluated the issue over decades, and the

---

[19] Haas, "Legitimacy of Neurological Criteria for the Determination of Death". Haas is himself a proponent of using neurological criteria to determine death. Regarding misdiagnoses, he writes: "Such cases of false declarations of brain death usually indicate the inadequate practice of medicine and do not negate the legitimacy of determining death by the use of neurological criteria, if it is done properly."

[20] Hanley, *Determining Death by Neurological Criteria*, 80.

[21] See a summary of those for and against the use of neurological criteria by Christopher Ostertag and Kyle Karches, "Brain Death and the Formation of Moral Conscience", *Linacre Quarterly* 86, no. 4 (November 2019), https://www.ncbi.nlm.nih.gov/pmc/articles/PMC6880067/.

[22] Ostertag and Karches, "Brain Death and the Formation of Moral Conscience".

body of magisterial teaching addressing the subject seems to favor accepting brain death as a legitimate definition of death (for cautions, see QQ. 40, 42, and 123).[23]

The Church definitively teaches that human death is "the separation of the soul from the body".[24] But, as Pope John Paul II acknowledged, death "is an event which no scientific technique or empirical method can identify directly".[25] He further stated: "With regard to the parameters used today for ascertaining death ... the Church does not make technical decisions. She limits herself to the Gospel duty of comparing the data offered by medical science with the Christian understanding of the unity of the person, bringing out the similarities and the possible conflicts capable of endangering respect for human dignity."[26]

What is clear is that determination of the death of a patient should be made by a "physician or competent medical authority in accordance with responsible and commonly accepted scientific criteria".[27] Currently, a determination of death is almost always defined and measured by one of two means: cardiopulmonary function or brain function (see Q. 39).

42. If my loved one previously expressed a desire to donate an organ and is subsequently declared

[23] See, for example, John Paul II, Transplantation Society, no. 5: "Here it can be said that the criterion adopted in more recent times for ascertaining the fact of death, namely the *complete* and *irreversible* cessation of all brain activity, if rigorously applied, does not seem to conflict with the essential elements of a sound anthropology" (emphasis in original).

[24] *Catechism of the Catholic Church*, no. 997.

[25] John Paul II, Transplantation Society, no. 5.

[26] John Paul II, Transplantation Society, no. 5.

[27] United States Conference of Catholic Bishops, *Ethical and Religious Directives for Catholic Health Care Services*, no. 62.

brain dead, is it moral to allow the organ to be taken?

Yes (but see Q. 40), assuming that the diagnosis of brain death is correct (that is, the neurological criteria were applied correctly and *irreversible* cessation (see Q. 39) of all functions of the entire brain has occurred).

The fact that a determination of death by neurological criteria (that is, brain death) can be made and organs can be harvested even though the patient's heart is beating is a reason for caution. In brain death it has become a common practice to harvest organs while the heart still beats; in cardiopulmonary death, organs are harvested minutes after the heart has irreversibly stopped beating. In the latter case, there is obviously less time to inspect and harvest organs.

To boost the number of organs from warm bodies, transplant surgeons have increasingly allowed terminal patients to die, before restarting their hearts and clamping off blood flow to the brain.[28] Known as "normothermic regional perfusion with controlled donation after circulatory death (NRP-cDCD)",[29] this disturbing practice of temporarily "reversing" cardiopulmonary death (that is, resuscitating a patient) to cause death by neurological criteria (brain death) strikes at the foundation of human dignity and raises serious questions about the moral vision of society. See Q. 123 for a fuller discussion of organ donation.

[28] See Randy Dotinga, "No Brain Death? No Problem. New Organ Transplant Protocol Stirs Debate", *MedPage Today*, September 28, 2022, https://www.medpagetoday.com/special-reports/exclusives/100950. "With little attention or debate, transplant surgeons across the country are experimenting with a kind of partial resurrection: They're allowing terminal patients to die, then restarting their hearts while clamping off blood flow to their brains. The procedure allows the surgeons to inspect and remove organs from warm bodies with heartbeats."

[29] Dotinga, "No Brain Death?". This procedure is growing, with hospitals in Nebraska, Arizona, and New York currently conducting clinical trials.

43. What are "suicide" and "physician-assisted suicide"?

Broadly speaking, suicide refers to the intentional taking of one's own life, and assisted suicide is suicide with the assistance of another person.

Physician-assisted suicide (often euphemistically called "medically assisted death" or "medical aid in dying") "occurs when a physician facilitates a patient's death by providing the necessary means and/or information to enable the patient to perform the life-ending act (e.g., the physician provides lethal medication, while aware that the patient may use such medication to commit suicide)".[30]

As of the date of publication of this book, nine states have allowed the practice of physician-assisted suicide either by popular vote (ballot initiative) or legislation: Oregon (1994), Washington (2008), Vermont (2013), California (2015), Colorado (2016), Hawaii (2018), New Jersey (2019), Maine (2019), and New Mexico (2021). Additionally, the Washington, DC, City Council (2016) passed a bill authorizing physician-assisted suicide in the nation's capital. Finally, the Supreme Court of Montana (2009), while not expressly recognizing a state constitutional right to physician-assisted suicide, held that the consent of a competent patient who seeks the assistance of a physician in committing suicide is a defense to a charge of assisting in that person's suicide.

44. What does the Church teach about suicide and assisted suicide?

The Church teaches that suicide is the intentional taking of one's own life and, as such, it "is always as morally

---

[30] "Opinion 5.7: Physician-Assisted Suicide", American Medical Association Code of Medical Ethics, accessed March 28, 2022, https://www.ama-assn.org /delivering-care/ethics/physician-assisted-suicide.

objectionable as murder".[31] The Church's constant teaching throughout history has been to reject suicide as a gravely evil choice. Saint Augustine observes, "In the holy canonical books, no divine precept or permission can be discovered which allows us to bring about our own death, either to obtain immortality or to avert or avoid some evil. On the contrary, we must understand the Law of God as forbidding us to do this, where it says, 'Thou shalt not kill.' "[32]

Although certain psychological and other factors may lessen or remove subjective responsibility, viewed objectively, suicide remains a gravely immoral act.[33] It involves "the rejection of the love of self and the renunciation of the obligation of justice and charity towards one's neighbor, towards the communities to which one belongs, and towards society as a whole".[34] These conclusions naturally flow from the understanding that we "are *stewards*, not owners, of the life God has entrusted us",[35] and that "God alone is the Lord of life from its beginning until its end: no one can under *any* circumstance claim for himself the right directly to destroy an innocent human being."[36]

45. What does the term "euthanasia" mean?

"Euthanasia" comes from a combination of Greek words meaning "good death" or "easy death". In ancient times it referred to death without severe suffering.[37] The old use of the term has been largely forgotten, however, and today, it

[31] John Paul II, *Evangelium vitae* (The Gospel of Life) (March 25, 1995), no. 66.

[32] Saint Augustine, *De Civitate Dei* I, 20, trans. and ed. R. W. Dyson (Cambridge: Cambridge University Press, 1998), 32.

[33] John Paul II, *Evangelium vitae*, no. 66.

[34] John Paul II, *Evangelium vitae*, no. 66.

[35] *Catechism of the Catholic Church*, no. 2280 (emphasis added).

[36] *Catechism of the Catholic Church*, no. 2258 (emphasis added).

[37] Congregation for the Doctrine of the Faith, *Declaration on Euthanasia* (May 5, 1980), section II.

is understood as "some intervention of medicine whereby the suffering of sickness or of the final agony are reduced, sometimes also with the danger of suppressing life prematurely. Ultimately, the word *Euthanasia* is used in a more particular sense to mean 'mercy killing' ".[38]

The idea of "mercy killing" is intended to convey the concept of "putting an end to extreme suffering, or [saving] abnormal babies, the mentally ill or the incurably sick from the prolongation, perhaps for many years of a miserable life, which could impose too heavy a burden on their families or society".[39]

In this book, "mercy killing" and "euthanasia" are used to mean an act or a failure to act "which of itself or by intention causes death, in order that all suffering may in this way be eliminated".[40] For an act or omission to be characterized as euthanasia, there must be an *intent* to kill the patient. It is essentially the same thing to take a concrete action to kill a patient or to fail to take a morally required action to preserve a patient's life, because the intent of the act or omission is to cause the patient's death.

46. What is the difference between "active euthanasia" and "passive euthanasia"?

Active euthanasia means that "someone intentionally chooses to kill a person by an act of commission",[41] which often occurs at the hands of a physician who administers lethal drugs to end an incurably or terminally ill patient's

[38] Congregation for the Doctrine of the Faith, *Declaration on Euthanasia*, section II.

[39] Congregation for the Doctrine of the Faith, *Declaration on Euthanasia*, section II.

[40] Congregation for the Doctrine of the Faith, *Declaration on Euthanasia*, section II.

[41] William E. May, *Catholic Bioethics and the Gift of Human Life* (Huntington, IN: Our Sunday Visitor, 2000), 238.

THE CHURCH'S TEACHING ON DEATH   87

life. Passive euthanasia means that someone, for (seemingly) merciful reasons, brings about the death of another by an act of omission.[42]

Although the categories are sometimes debated, from the perspective of consent, there are three types of active and passive euthanasia: *voluntary* (at the patient's request), *nonvoluntary* (without patient consent, generally due to inability), and *involuntary* (the patient refuses consent).[43]

47. What does the Catholic Church teach about active and passive euthanasia?

It is always immoral to engage in euthanasia. The Catholic Church teaches that euthanasia "in the strict sense is understood to be an action or omission which of itself and by intention causes death",[44] usually with the purpose of either eliminating the suffering of some person who is at the terminal stages of his life or is deemed to have a life not worth living because of some perceived disability. As such, euthanasia "is a *crime against human life* because, in this act, one chooses directly to cause the death of another innocent human being".[45]

48. I want to help my loved one die to stop his suffering. How can that be wrong?

Even when euthanasia is motivated by a desire to extend mercy, the Church recognizes that it is a "false mercy" and

---

[42] May, *Catholic Bioethics*, 239.

[43] See D. V. K. Chao, N. Y. Chan, and W. Y. Chan, "Euthanasia Revisited", *Family Practice* 19, no. 2 (April 2002), https://academic.oup.com/fampra/article/19/2/128/490935?login=false.

[44] John Paul II, *Evangelium vitae*, no. 65.

[45] Congregation for the Doctrine of the Faith, *Letter "Samaritanus bonus" of the Congregation for the Doctrine of the Faith on the Care of Persons in the Critical and Terminal Phases of Life* (September 22, 2020), section I.

a " 'perversion' of mercy".[46] As the Congregation for the Doctrine of the Faith's letter *Samaritanus bonus* affirms, "In reality, human compassion consists not in causing death, but in embracing the sick, in supporting them in their difficulties, in offering them affection, attention, and the means to alleviate the suffering."[47]

The principle of intention is fundamental in making good end-of-life decisions. A good intention is a necessary element of a moral act (see Q. 100), but a good intention cannot save an intrinsically evil act (see QQ. 96–100).

The Church's teachings are clear that "an act or omission which, of itself or by intention, causes death to eliminate suffering constitutes a murder gravely contrary to the dignity of the human person and to the respect due to the living God, his Creator. The error of judgment into which one can fall in good faith does not change the nature of this murderous act, which must always be forbidden and excluded."[48]

---

[46] John Paul II, *Evangelium vitae*, nos. 65, 66.

[47] Congregation for the Doctrine of the Faith, *Samaritanus bonus*, section IV.

[48] *Catechism of the Catholic Church*, no. 2277 (quoting Congregation for the Doctrine of the Faith, *Donum vitae* [February 22, 1987], I, 6).

IV

HINDRANCES TO MORAL
DECISION-MAKING AT
THE END OF LIFE

49. Isn't my common sense enough to guide me in making good moral decisions?

No. Common sense isn't all that common these days, and its exercise is prone to subjective error. Also, what we customarily mean when we use the term "common sense" is too ambiguous to provide an objective standard for moral decision-making.

Any discussion about morality requires a clear standard for determining what right and wrong are. If a standard is to help us distinguish between good and evil decisions and actions, it must consider the truth about man—his nature and destiny—and it must provide us with fixed, uniform, and universal norms that allow no exceptions. In short, we must have an objective standard to distinguish right from wrong.

50. Can't I just follow my conscience?

Everyone is responsible for following his conscience, whether it commands or forbids some action, but the question of conscience in moral decision-making requires a fuller explanation.

Unfortunately, in recent decades in the Catholic Church, the concept of conscience has been misused by those who dissent from the authoritative teachings of the Church in preference for their own opinions. This began in full force with dissent from the Church's constant teaching against artificial contraception, confirmed by Pope Paul VI in the 1960s. A misguided appeal to conscience has now come to serve as a shield for many immoral acts.[1] Used in this way, conscience appears to mean one's autonomous opinion or desire uninformed by the Church's perennial teaching. In essence, it is a refusal of submission to any authority above oneself.

In reality, the conscience is neither our subjective impressions of right and wrong nor the slavish, unthinking submission to the directions of ecclesiastical leaders.[2] It is an act of reason and judgment by which a person uses his mind to apply his knowledge of right and wrong to a specific course of action.[3] A person's decision in a given case depends on the guiding principles already in that person's mind.[4] The conscience is the internal rule of human acts, but it needs an external guide. This external guide comes from the moral law (see QQ. 88–92).

If someone's conscience is well-formed—that is, if the guiding principles present in his mind are morally sound—and he follows those principles, he will make a morally good decision. If the principles are unsound (that is, either unreasonable or contrary to the Church's teachings) or clouded by emotion or poor counsel, he is likely to make a morally bad decision.

51. I thought my conscience was simply what I believed in my heart to be right. If not, what is it?

[1] In current usage, this shield often covers immoral opinions and acts dealing with sexual sins and offenses against the dignity of marriage and chastity (sixth commandment) and the interior disposition of improper sexual desire (ninth commandment).

[2] An excellent treatment of conscience in obedience to the Church's teachings and ecclesiastical leaders is Peter Kwasniewski's *True Obedience in the Church: A Guide to Discernment in Challenging Times* (Manchester, NH: Sophia Institute Press, 2021), 43–51. There are many fuller treatments of conscience generally, but we are indebted to and recommend Kwasniewski's work as a model of clarity, brevity, and succinctness in responding to this question.

[3] See *Catechism of the Catholic Church*, no. 1778.

[4] John Hardon, *Modern Catholic Dictionary* (Garden City, NY: Doubleday, 1980), s.v. "Conscience", 126.

It is a common but unfortunate belief of some that one's conscience is merely one's interior opinion of right and wrong. If this were so, there would be few cases of a person having a bad or troubled conscience or a conscience that could be cleansed.

Our conscience is not our interior opinions, feelings, sentiments, or intuition or merely a habituated way of thinking. It is an act of *judgment* governed by the moral law, especially natural law (see Q. 90). It is a specific act of the mind that applies knowledge to particular circumstances to decide on a course of action.

A good definition of conscience, from Father John Hardon, is "The judgment of the practical intellect deciding, from general principles of faith and reason, the goodness or badness of a way of acting that a person now faces."[5]

52. If he is certain, isn't a Christian free to follow his conscience in end-of-life decisions?

A Christian ought to follow his conscience, but freedom and conscience are subject to an external guide that is truth.[6] Conscience must never be understood as a license to form the moral opinions one likes. Certainty may be understood as the psychological conviction with which one holds an opinion or viewpoint.[7] Since it is possible to reach a level of psychological certainty even about wrong viewpoints, it is critical to have a true conscience. Dominic M. Prümmer writes that a conscience "is *true* (correct) when it deduces correctly from true principles that some act is lawful; it is *false* (erroneous) when it decides from

---

[5] Hardon, *Modern Catholic Dictionary*, s.v. "Conscience", 126.

[6] See *Catechism of the Catholic Church*, no. 1777.

[7] Peter E. Bristow, *The Moral Dignity of Man* (Dublin, Ireland: Four Courts Press, 1997), 63–64.

false principles *considered as true* that something is lawful which in fact is unlawful."[8]

53. Can my conscience ever mislead me?

Yes, conscience is not infallible. It may make mistakes, just like any other human judgment. Since conscience is an act of judgment, it is also possible to set it aside. For example, the natural law is written in every man's conscience (see Q. 90), telling him that murder is wrong, but men do lay aside that common judgment and commit murder. The *Catechism* tells us, "Faced with a moral choice, conscience can make either a right judgment in accordance with reason and the divine law or, on the contrary, an erroneous judgment that departs from them."[9]

The judgment of conscience, if set aside, can become defiled (see 1 Cor 8:7). If it is persistently set aside, it becomes hardened or seared (see 1 Tim 4:2). Referring to the coming fate of the apostles, Jesus said, "They will put you out of the synagogues; indeed, the hour is coming when whoever kills you will think he is offering service to God" (Jn 16:2).

It is also possible to have a lax conscience, which is a conscience that erroneously judges an act or decision to be harmless when, in fact, it is a serious sin.[10] A lax conscience can result from poor instruction or formation, neglecting or minimizing the Church's moral teachings, or neglecting

[8] Dominic M. Prümmer, O.P., *Handbook of Moral Theology*, trans. Gerald W. Shelton (Manchester, NH: Benedictus Books, 2022), 61 (emphasis in original). Prümmer notes that "the means to be used for obtaining a true conscience are a) a careful knowledge of the laws which govern our moral life; b) taking wise counsel; c) prayer to the Father of light; d) removal of obstacles to a true conscience, chief amongst which is the obscurity resulting from unforgiven sin." *Handbook*, 62.

[9] *Catechism of the Catholic Church*, no. 1786.

[10] Henry Davis, S.J., *Moral and Pastoral Theology*, ed. L. W. Geddes (New York: Sheed and Ward, 1959), 1:77.

to correct wrong personal opinions when they are pointed out. Essentially, a lax conscience is rooted in the principle of private judgment—that is, the tendency to prefer one's own opinions to the teaching of the Church in matters of faith and morals.[11]

If our conscience misleads us, it is often through practical neglect of moral truths, followed by a tendency to justify oneself.[12] Before long, the first principles of natural law and moral reasoning are obscured, which prompts doubt and an inability to apply moral principles in concrete situations.

Thus, while a Christian is free and must follow his conscience, he also must form his conscience in accordance with right reason and the Church's constant teaching regarding the moral law and moral decision-making.

54. How does my conscience properly work in making moral decisions?

A person with a properly formed conscience—one with a firm grasp of principles of reason and the moral law—applies his knowledge of what is right and wrong, what is appropriate and inappropriate, to the concrete circumstances he faces. He considers and weighs his possible actions in light of his knowledge and makes a reasoned decision consistent with the moral law. But the conclusion he reaches depends on the guiding principles already in his mind when he is called upon to decide between right and wrong.

This process underscores the critical importance of sound moral formation.[13] Insofar as a man is formed in what is right and wrong for his nature (the moral law for a moral nature in the image of God), he is psychologically

[11] Davis, *Moral and Pastoral Theology*, 1:78.
[12] Davis, *Moral and Pastoral Theology*, 1:64.
[13] See *Catechism of the Catholic Church*, no. 1783.

and morally sound. His conscience thus enables him to understand the principles of morality and the moral law, apply those principles to concrete circumstances, and make a morally good judgment.

55. The formation of my conscience seems difficult and complex. Is it even possible?

Yes, the sound formation of conscience is possible and attainable by any Catholic who is capable of understanding right and wrong.

Admittedly, it is conceivable that one might presume when approaching this book that the process of moral formation and moral reasoning is highly complex and time-consuming. But it is not. All Catholics are called to virtue in their daily life in Christ. Catholics who take this call seriously seek to grow in and live in the virtues consistently.[14] This process, over time, if engaged in consistently according to a sound rule of life life, results in the illumination of conscience. In short, if one seeks God and strives with his help to live a life of virtue, one's conscience tends to conform to the moral law.

In the life of a "virtuous person with an illumined mind",[15] moral reasoning and decision-making are constantly taking

[14] Perennial Catholic teaching recognizes three theological virtues—faith, hope, and charity—which "are infused by God into the souls of the faithful [at baptism] to make them capable of acting as his children" (*Catechism of the Catholic Church*, no. 1813). An infused virtue is one given by God supernaturally in the soul without one's effort. In addition to the theological virtues, there are four cardinal, or moral, virtues: prudence, justice, fortitude, and temperance. Our efforts acquire these moral virtues, whose purpose is living a good life. In his goodness, however, God has elevated the natural virtues by his grace in the life of Christians (*Catechism of the Catholic Church*, no. 1810). These natural virtues practiced in the power of God's grace help us meet our natural good and our ultimate good—eternal bliss with Christ in heaven.

[15] Peter Kwasniewski, *True Obedience in the Church: A Guide to Discernment in Challenging Times* (Manchester, NH: Sophia Institute Press, 2021), 51.

place. As a result of his formation, certain decisions seem natural and prove to be very easy. Other decisions, like some moral decisions at the end of life, require specific instruction from the Church's teachings to provide Catholics with the principles of faith that apply and that will help the person decide the "goodness or badness" of the decision before him in a concrete situation.

Among the various means to help correctly form one's conscience, there are several that bear emphasizing. The U.S. Catholic bishops write, "Each baptized follower of Christ is obliged to form his or her conscience according to objective moral standards. The Word of God is a principal tool in the formation of conscience when it is assimilated by study, prayer, and practice.... The authoritative teaching of the Church is an essential element in our conscience formation."[16] In Appendix II, the authors make specific suggestions for an approach to spiritual and moral formation.

56. I am concerned with the decline of my "quality of life". Isn't that the most crucial factor to consider in making decisions about serious illness and the end of life?

No, it is not the most crucial factor. First, nothing is wrong with wanting to live physically fit and mentally vibrant lives until our last hour. Neither is there anything wrong with wanting to remain a benefit to family and society for as long as we live. To desire such a good quality of life is not only not inherently wrong but also perfectly reasonable.

[16] "Morality", United States Conference of Catholic Bishops, excerpted from *United States Catholic Catechism for Adults* (Washington, DC: United States Catholic Conference of Bishops, 2006), accessed March 8, 2022, https://www.usccb.org/beliefs-and-teachings/what-we-believe/morality.

Unfortunately, however, the term "quality of life" has often been co-opted in end-of-life contexts and appropriated for a sinister purpose. In such contexts, modern proponents of voluntary euthanasia sometimes aggressively advance the concept to argue that with some who are seriously ill, their quality of life has decreased to the point that life itself is no longer worth living. Thus, to choose to end one's life or to assist someone in ending his own life is considered a merciful act that serves as a relief from a burdensome and entirely useless life.[17]

Quality of life, properly understood, may be a *consideration* in making certain end-of-life decisions (see Q. 58), but the concept should never be used to conclude that life is not worth living. Moreover, quality of life judgments are notoriously arbitrary. What precisely are the various qualities that make a life meaningful as we age? The possibilities are almost endless, and so are the moral dangers (see Q. 57).

57. What are the dangers in considering the quality of life to make end-of-life decisions?

The danger comes from the modern presuppositions about the qualities that make life worth living. In our modern society, people tend to assume that qualities like pleasure, painless health, economic well-being, and the like are the qualities that make life worth living. Thus, when those qualities diminish, a person with such presuppositions can unreasonably conclude that he would be better off if he were no longer alive.

Pope John Paul II, in the encyclical *Evangelium vitae*, insightfully discloses the transparent presuppositions that tend to undergird the modern quality of life argument:

---

[17] William E. May, *Catholic Bioethics and the Gift of Human Life* (Huntington, IN: Our Sunday Visitor, 2000), 249.

When the prevailing tendency is to value life only to the extent that it brings pleasure and well-being, suffering seems like an unbearable setback, something from which one must be freed at all costs. Death is considered "senseless" if it suddenly interrupts a life still open to a future of new and interesting experiences. But it becomes a "rightful liberation" once life is held to be no longer meaningful because it is filled with pain and inexorably doomed to even greater suffering.[18]

When viewed from this perspective, the presuppositions that tend to drive the modern view of quality of life in relation to euthanasia are virtually atheistic. They tend to discount or ignore the loving providence of God in the circumstances of individual lives. The presuppositions overlook or deny the deeper meaning of suffering, and in particular, they lead one to miss the opportunity afforded by aging and sickness to share in Christ's redemptive sufferings (see Q. 63).

58. From a Catholic perspective, is there any place for considering the quality of life in decision-making at the end of life?

As noted above (Q. 56), it is normal to desire a good quality of life. In our current context, however, where we face an "extraordinary increase and gravity of threats"[19] against the aging, there are risks to focusing on the quality of life when making end-of-life decisions. Nonetheless, one can consider quality of life in a way that accords with Catholic moral teaching. For example, there are sometimes circumstances of illness—age, diagnosis, aggressiveness and burdens of treatment, and risks—that may counsel a patient

[18] John Paul II, encyclical letter *Evangelium vitae* (The Gospel of Life) (March 25, 1995), no. 64.
[19] John Paul II, *Evangelium vitae*, no. 3.

to decline interventions as extraordinary and burdensome, thus deciding in favor of a higher quality of life even if it results in a shorter life. The Church's moral teaching helps determine when such a decision is appropriate (see Part VII on the moral law).

59. My seriously ill loved one was presented with the hospital's Futility of Care Policy upon admission. What does that mean?

Regrettably, hospitals and medical associations in the United States and Canada have quietly adopted formal "futile care" policies.[20] Such policies can be used by hospitals, despite the objections of patients or families, to deny care to persons with a debilitating or terminal disease because a physician or medical provider believes further medical care to be futile.

The problem with futile care policies is that they involve "subjective value judgments by medical professionals rather than physiological outcomes".[21] The meaning and guidelines for a futility of care or medical futility determination, as it is also known, have long been disputed in the medical, legal, and ethical professions.[22] Some have gone so far as to assert that "a definition continues to elude the medical profession."[23] This ambiguity leads naturally

[20] Wesley J. Smith, "Who Decides When Care Is Futile?" *National Post*, November 23, 1998, reprinted by Catholic Education Resource Center, https://www.catholiceducation.org/en/controversy/euthanasia-and-assisted-suicide/who-decides-when-care-is-futile.html.

[21] Smith, "Who Decides?".

[22] Peter A. Clark, S.J., "Medical Futility: Medical and Ethical Analysis", *Virtual Mentor* 9, no. 5 (May 2007), https://journalofethics.ama-assn.org/article/medical-futility-legal-and-ethical-analysis/2007-05.

[23] See, e.g., Rebecca Pieknik, "The Challenges of Medical Futility", *The Surgical Technologist* (August 2003), https://www.ast.org/articles/2003/2003-08-233.pdf.

to the possibility that futility of care will mean different things to different medical professionals.[24]

What can and often does happen is not only that those medical professionals cease treatments that no longer provide any benefit to the patient, but also that their subjective values lead them to discontinue further therapies or interventions that *do* benefit the patient. For example, a ventilator may be turned off not because it is not helping a patient, but precisely because it is helping him and thus might allow him to continue a life that a medical professional has subjectively determined is no longer worth continuing.[25] In such a case, the possibility of grave moral error and destruction to the dignity of human beings is difficult to exaggerate.

As Dr. Deborah L. Kasman has well stated, "*medical CARE is NEVER futile.*"[26] Certain treatments may be of little or no benefit to a patient, but medical *care* is not. The United States Conference of Catholic Bishops noted, "The task of medicine is to care even when it cannot cure."[27]

Given the current ambiguity in the concept of the futility of care and documented cases of its subjective application by medical professionals, it is advisable to be highly cautious in basing end-of-life decisions on the conclusion

[24] See, e.g., John Botha, Ravindranath Tiruvoipati, and David Goldberg, "Futility of Medical Treatment in Current Medical Practice", *The New Zealand Medical Journal* 126, no. 1383 (September 2013), where the authors' definition of futility of care is so broad and susceptible to subjectivity as to render the concept of limited value: "The medical literature currently refers to futile care as care that is physiologically, qualitatively, or quantitatively futile."

[25] Botha, Tiruvoipati, and Goldberg, "Futility of Medical Treatment".

[26] Deborah L. Kasman, "When Is Medical Treatment Futile? A Guide for Students, Residents, and Physicians", *Journal of General Internal Medicine* 19, no. 10 (October 2004), https://pubmed.ncbi.nlm.nih.gov/15482559/ (emphasis in original).

[27] United States Conference of Catholic Bishops, *Ethical and Religious Directives for Catholic Health Care Services*, no. 29.

that further care is futile. When a physician, patient, or family believes medical treatments are futile, there should be a respectful process of discussion and negotiation, informed and guided by Catholic moral teaching.

60. I don't want to be a burden near the end of my life. Shouldn't I be free to make any end-of-life decision that will prevent that?

No, not just any decision. Basing end-of-life decisions on the perception that one is a burden is a danger to moral decision-making and thus a danger to the soul.[28] Unfortunately, studies indicate that the fear of being a burden to loved ones is a significant factor in patients' decisions to seek assisted suicide or euthanasia.[29] But the self-perception behind such decisions is distorted and needs to be reconsidered in light of our nature and how God sees us (see Part V).

We are created in the image of God, and every human life is sacred and in a special relationship with God. Our lives in themselves can thus never be a burden to others. However, there are terms frequently used in end-of-life decision-making that can lead to confusion on this issue if not carefully considered—terms like "burdensome prolongation of life" and "excessive burden".[30]

---

[28] In reality, in Catholic thought and teaching, the very idea that the existence and life of a human being could be a burden is deplorable and should always be discouraged. The idea is of pagan origin rather than Christian.

[29] See, e.g., Paschal M. Corby, OFM Conv., "The Fear of Being a Burden on Others: A Response to the Rhetoric of Euthanasia and Assisted Suicide", *The National Catholic Bioethics Quarterly* 19, no. 3 (Autumn 2019).

[30] The use of phrases that incorporate the word "burden" is unfortunate and ought to be reconsidered or refined due to ambiguity. Such use unintentionally lends itself to modern confusion regarding the value of human life. Nonetheless, the Church's use of these and similar terms refers more to things not required by the moral law when considered in light of the benefit they provide to a patient. They do not refer to and must be carefully distinguished

It is essential to understand that these terms do not refer to a person's value or any burden a patient's continued existence in itself has on others. They are simply terms intended to help determine whether a treatment or refusal of treatment is proportionate or disproportionate. There is a moral option for Catholics with a terminal illness to forgo disproportionate or extraordinary treatments that offer no reasonable hope of benefit.[31] Thus, terms like "burdensome prolongation of life" and "excessive burden", if part of a careful analysis of a patient's concrete circumstances, can help determine a moral course of action (see QQ. 26–28 for further explanation of burdensome prolongation of life and excessive burden).

61. Are pain and suffering the same thing?

No. It is important to have a basic understanding of this distinction between pain and suffering as a corrective to the idea that all suffering is meaningless. "Pain" and "suffering" are sometimes used interchangeably, but there is a distinction. This distinction comes from the fact that a human being is both body and soul (see Q. 35). When the body suffers physical discomfort, it is in pain. Suffering is a reaction to pain and includes both a physical and a moral dimension. It is the "experience of soul that comes with the presence of evil or the privation of some good".[32] Theologically speaking, suffering, whether physical or

---

from conclusions that a person has reached a point when his further existence is a drain or burden on others. The Church's intention is to provide a practical means of analyzing the benefits and burdens of treatment.

[31] United States Conference of Catholic Bishops, *Ethical and Religious Directives for Catholic Health Care Services*, no. 57.

[32] See Hardon, *Modern Catholic Dictionary*, s.v. "Suffering", 523; see also John Paul II, apostolic letter *Salvifici doloris* (On the Christian Meaning of Human Suffering) (February 11, 1984), no. 5: "*Physical suffering* is present when 'the body is hurting' in some way, whereas *moral suffering* is 'pain of the soul'" (emphasis in original).

moral, is the result of sin entering the world in the Fall. Thus, a person suffers whenever he experiences any physical or moral evil.[33]

62. What are the spiritual opportunities suffering offers us?

Suffering is a providential opportunity to unite oneself with Christ, to express praise and love, and to discover the salvific meaning of suffering.[34] Suffering comes to us as a trial that can either lead us away from God[35] or lead us into a deeper sharing of Christ's sufferings (see 2 Cor 4:8–11; Phil 3:10–11; Col 1:24); it can also provoke "a search for God and a return to him".[36] As the Catholic Church teaches: "In illness, man experiences his powerlessness, his limitations, and his finitude. Every illness can make us glimpse death."[37]

Suffering, although the result of the Fall, has a purpose in this life. It is a means to "expiate wrongdoing" and to "enable the believer to offer God a sacrifice of praise ... to unite oneself with Christ in his sufferings as an expression of love, and in the process to become more like

[33] John Paul II, *Salvifici doloris*, no. 7.

[34] See John Paul II, *Salvifici doloris*, no. 1, commenting on St. Paul's declaration of the power of salvific suffering in Colossians 1:24: "In my flesh I complete what is lacking in Christ's afflictions for the sake of his body, that is, the Church". Pope John Paul II writes: "These words have as it were the value of a final discovery, which is accompanied by joy. For this reason Saint Paul writes: 'Now I rejoice in my sufferings for your sake.' The joy comes from the discovery of the meaning of suffering, and this discovery, even if it is most personally shared in by Paul of Tarsus who wrote these words, is at the same time valid for others. The Apostle shares his own discovery and rejoices in it because of all those whom it can help—just as it helped him—to understand *the salvific meaning of suffering*" (emphasis in original).

[35] See *Catechism of the Catholic Church*, no. 1501.

[36] See *Catechism of the Catholic Church*, no. 1501.

[37] *Catechism of the Catholic Church*, no. 1500.

Christ, who having joy set before him, chose the cross, and thus 'to make up all that has still to be undergone by Christ for the sake of his body, the Church' (Col 1:24)"[38] (for a focused discussion on the redemptive power of suffering, see Q. 63).

Suffering, while not good in itself, can awaken us from sin, apathy, and self-absorption and serve as a means of bringing us into a deeper relationship with Christ. C. S. Lewis alluded to this spiritual power of suffering when he wrote: "Pain insists upon being attended to. God whispers to us in our pleasures, speaks in our conscience, but shouts in our pain: it is His megaphone to rouse a deaf world."[39] Pope John Paul II wrote, "Suffering must serve *for conversion*, that is, *for the rebuilding of goodness* in the subject, who can recognize the divine mercy in this call to repentance."[40] Especially when accompanied by sickness and aging and its attendant humiliations, suffering is an invitation to turn away from fear and self-absorption—to repentance and conversion, faith and love.

By enduring and embracing the cross of suffering, we may merit an eternal reward. Saint Paul says, "We ourselves boast of you ... for your steadfastness and faith in all your persecutions and in the afflictions which you are enduring. This is evidence of the righteous judgment of God, that you may be made worthy of the kingdom of God, for which you are suffering" (2 Thes 1:4–5).

63. How can we participate by our suffering in Christ's redemption?

---

[38] Hardon, *Modern Catholic Dictionary*, s.v. "Suffering", 523.

[39] C. S. Lewis, *The Problem of Pain* (New York: HarperCollins, 2001), 91.

[40] John Paul II, *Salvici doloris*, no. 12 (emphasis in original).

The Holy Scriptures teach that we share in Christ's sufferings because we are joined to him as members of his body.[41] The Church has perpetually taught the mystery that Christ is aided by the members of his body in carrying out the work of redemption, not because his work is ineffective in any way, but instead because he willed it for the glory of his spouse, the Church. Moreover, Christ wills that the salvation of many depends on the prayers and voluntary penances of the members of his body. As Pope Pius XII makes clear:

> He has so willed it for the greater glory of His spotless Spouse. Dying on the Cross He left to His Church the immense treasury of the Redemption, towards which she contributed nothing. But when those graces come to be distributed, not only does He share this work of sanctification with His Church, but He wills that in some way it be due to her action. This is a deep mystery, and an inexhaustible subject of meditation, that the salvation of many depends on the prayers and voluntary penances which the members of the Mystical Body of Jesus Christ offer for this intention and on the cooperation of pastors of souls and of the faithful, especially of fathers and mothers of families, a cooperation which they must offer to our Divine Savior as though they were His associates.[42]

[41] See, e.g., 1 Cor 12:12, 26–27: "For just as the body is one and has many members, and all the members of the body, though many, are one body, so it is with Christ.... If one member suffers, all suffer together; if one member is honored, all rejoice together. Now you are the body of Christ and individually members of it"; 2 Cor 1:5: "For as we share abundantly in Christ's sufferings, so through Christ we share abundantly in comfort too"; 2 Cor 4:8–12: "We are afflicted in every way, but not crushed; perplexed, but not driven to despair; persecuted, but not forsaken; struck down, but not destroyed; always carrying in the body the death of Jesus, so that the life of Jesus may also be manifested in our bodies. For while we live we are always being given up to death for Jesus' sake, so that the life of Jesus may be manifested in our mortal flesh."

[42] Pius XII, encyclical letter *Mystici Corporis Christi* (On the Mystical Body of Christ) (June 29, 1943), no. 44.

The fact that we are joined to Christ means that our sufferings are united with his, and in this way, we participate in the redemption he accomplished. Pope John Paul II put it this way:

> The Redeemer suffered in place of man and for man. Every man has *his own share in the Redemption*. Each one is also *called to share in that suffering* through which the Redemption was accomplished. He is called to share in that suffering through which all human suffering has also been redeemed. In bringing about the Redemption through suffering, Christ *has* also *raised human suffering to the level of the Redemption*. Thus each man, in his suffering, can also become a sharer in the redemptive suffering of Christ.[43]

The victory over sin and death achieved by Christ in his death and Resurrection throws a new light "upon every suffering: the light of salvation".[44] Pope Leo XIII says that Christ did not take away pains and sorrows in this life but

> transformed them into motives of virtue and occasions of merit; and no man can hope for eternal reward unless he follow in the blood-stained footprints of his Saviour. "If we suffer with Him, we shall also reign with Him." Christ's labors and sufferings, accepted of His own free will, have marvellously sweetened all suffering and all labor. And not only by His example, but by His grace and by the hope held forth of everlasting recompense, has He made pain and grief more easy to endure; "for that which is at present momentary and light of our tribulation, worketh for us above measure exceedingly an eternal weight of glory."[45]

[43] John Paul II, *Salvifici doloris*, no. 19 (emphasis in original).
[44] John Paul II, *Salvifici doloris*, no. 15.
[45] Leo XIII, encyclical letter *Rerum Novarum* (On Capital and Labor) (May 15, 1891), no. 21 (quoting 2 Tim 2:12 and 2 Cor 4:17).

Christian suffering has an infinite value if it is joined with Christ's suffering, death, and Resurrection. Not only did Christ redeem mankind from sin and death, but human suffering has a continuing positive effect in this life if accepted with humility and joined to Christ's suffering at the foot of the Cross. John Paul II points out: "In the Cross of Christ not only is the Redemption accomplished through suffering, but *also human suffering itself has been redeemed.*"[46]

64. Can fear of suffering distort our thinking about end-of-life decision-making?

Yes. Despite the Church's constant teaching that suffering can be the antechamber of great happiness, if considered only in itself, suffering can cloud a person's thinking during serious illness. Making the avoidance of suffering the sole priority in end-of-life decision-making is a mistake. Suffering is neither pointless nor meaningless.

Also, suffering is not the rare interruption of an otherwise happy and difficulty-free life in this world. It is a reality of every human life and takes on even greater meaning for the follower of Christ. That greater meaning comes from the knowledge that God graciously guides all things in our lives in a way that maintains our freedom. Thus, when God allows us to suffer, he either protects us from a greater evil or leads us to a greater good. He always has a higher purpose in allowing suffering, even when that purpose is unclear to us. The priority of every Catholic is always to glorify God and to make his way to heaven, and unavoidable pain and suffering can aid in achieving that priority.

Some people consider physician-assisted suicide or euthanasia from a lack of understanding concerning the

[46]John Paul II, *Salvici doloris*, no. 19 (emphasis in original).

basic moral principles of end-of-life decision-making. Some are unaware that such decisions are moral and have profound spiritual ramifications. And some people are simply fearful of the mystery of death and the process of dying.

Serious illness and dying often create powerful anxieties that make even Christians vulnerable to seeking physician-assisted suicide or euthanasia, but fear of suffering as a basis for decision-making must always be resisted. In end-of-life decisions, as with all decisions, it must be kept in mind that any action motivated and driven by fear cannot be a moral decision, for what a person does from fear is done by compulsion and is therefore not a voluntary act—for any action to be moral, it must be free and voluntary.

Many fear dying in severe pain at the end of life and suffering without adequate means of controlling pain. Some, especially older adults, have distressing memories of loved ones dying of disease in significant pain. Unaware of the modern medical advances in pain management, some go so far as to express sentiments such as "I would rather die by my own hand than suffer excruciating pain" (suicide); "I would rather be put out of my misery if I am suffering terribly" (euthanasia); or, "We treat animals better than we do human beings at the end of life" (viewing human life as no more significant than animal life).

Such sentiments reveal fear and near despair at the thought of pain and suffering as death grows near, which can lead otherwise faithful Catholics to pursue immoral solutions at the end of life that undermine the inherent dignity of all human life and endanger their immortal souls.

65. Does the Christian understanding of the value of suffering mean we are required to experience and endure pain at the end of life?

No. It is a normal human desire to avoid pain and suffering, but pain and suffering are often unavoidable. In the words of Pope John Paul II, suffering is *"almost inseparable from man's earthly existence"*.[47] Pain and suffering in serious illness is both a trial and an opportunity. While it is not wrong to desire to avoid pain and suffering, it is essential to prepare ahead of serious illness to enter more fully into Christ's sufferings rather than turning inward in fear and self-absorption.

It is an unfortunate misrepresentation sometimes directed at the Catholic Church that it unsympathetically expects people at the terminal stages of life to experience and endure pain instead of alleviating it. On the contrary, the Church directs that those patients in the last setting of life "should be kept as free of pain as possible so they may die comfortably and with dignity".[48]

The Church does recognize as praiseworthy the occasional heroic soul who voluntarily accepts suffering, sometimes to the point of forgoing pain medications. Still, Pope John Paul II made clear that "such 'heroic' behaviour cannot be considered the duty of everyone".[49] Catholics are called to live lives of sanctity and virtue, but that call does not require patients experiencing terrible pain to suffer without help.

We are not expected simply to endure pain and suffering in our last stage of life with no attempt to alleviate it, and most of us do everything we can to avoid pain, suffering, or discomfort. For Christians, however, it is critical to remember that our suffering is not pointless. It drives us to God, and it can be redemptive when offered up to God

[47] John Paul II, *Salvifici doloris*, no. 3 (emphasis in original).
[48] United States Conference of Catholic Bishops, *Ethical and Religious Directives for Catholic Health Care Services*, no. 61.
[49] John Paul II, *Evangelium vitae*, no. 65.

as a sacrifice for our sake and the sake of others. Even though suffering is not inherently good, it can *produce* good if we endure with God's help what we cannot avoid, allow it to purify us, and unite it with the perfect sacrifice of Christ.

66. Since long illnesses can result in economic hardship or ruin, is it wrong to make end-of-life decisions based on fear of dying penniless?

Yes. Concern for finances is normal, but a decision made from fear is made under compulsion and is therefore not a free and voluntary moral decision—for any act to be moral, it must be free and voluntary.

As medical technology has advanced, so have its costs. A widely discussed statistic is that the average person incurs half of all the medical costs he will ever accrue in the last six months of his life. It is thus no wonder that many people fear that a medical calamity will wipe out their hard-earned savings and render them penniless. Economic considerations are thus not unimportant in end-of-life decision-making, and the Church provides helpful guidance in determining their role (see QQ. 28–29). Fear and economic costs *alone*, however, are not adequate reasons to guide end-of-life decisions. If decisions are driven by fear or cost becomes the sole criterion in end-of-life decisions, a patient or a patient's family may make an immoral decision with serious spiritual consequences.

67. What about the fear of dying alone?

God is always present with us, and, as Christians, we are to do everything in our power to ensure no one ever dies without the aid and prayers of others. This is especially true of our duty to love members of the Catholic faithful. "Do good to all men, and especially to those who are of the household of faith" (Gal 6:10). Unfortunately, people sometimes die without friends and loved ones to help them in their passing. It is understandable that these people, Catholics included, fear dying alone so much that they are vulnerable to being misled by the siren song of physician-assisted suicide and euthanasia.

The reality of hospice care is a blessing in helping family and friends provide care and companionship at the end of life. Hospice care, whether at home or in a facility, offers specialized care for people suffering from terminal illness. Properly understood, a hospice is not so much a place as a commitment to providing comfort care wherever the patient considers home. The focus is on caring when curing a patient is no longer an option. Specifically, the emphasis in hospice is usually on pain and symptom relief combined with providing spiritual nourishment to the dying, including the sacraments and personal counseling (for more on hospice care, see Q. 33).

68. The thought of losing my freedom is overwhelming; is it wrong to be concerned with maintaining the autonomy to make my own decisions about how my life will end?

It depends upon what is meant by the term "autonomy" and the decisions one believes himself free to make. There is a legitimate form of autonomy (see Q. 70), but the fear of losing autonomy at the end of life may be due to an unwitting embrace of a false idea of autonomy—whereby each person has the right to determine and impose the moral law on himself and each person is in control of his own life, including the conditions surrounding his death.

Like several concepts in moral decision-making, terms must be carefully defined. The English word "autonomy" comes from the Greek words *auto* (self) and *nomos* (law). Moral autonomy, more commonly known simply as autonomy, is "the theory that each person imposes the moral law on himself"[50] without interference from external forces; in short, man is his own source of moral law.

Pope Pius XII reminds us that "man is only the custodian, not the independent possessor and owner of his body, his life, and of all that the Creator has given to him."[51] Human autonomy and freedom are not unlimited. They must be guided by truth, and the truth ultimately comes from God and the moral law.

The idea of autonomy that drives people to consider physician-assisted suicide is the type that claims radical freedom, even from God and the moral law. The argument is that a person is merely exercising his autonomy when he gives free and informed consent to being "mercifully" killed.[52] It is quickly becoming the prevailing view that it would be a lack of respect for a person's autonomy to interfere with such a decision and that, in fact, respect requires that the person be assisted in exercising his autonomy if he so chooses. He is not to be interfered with by any external forces.

Since we are created by God, we are dependent upon him to sustain us. We are therefore never autonomous from him, nor are we free to decide our own moral standards. The term "autonomy", as it is popularly used, courts

[50] See Hardon, *Modern Catholic Dictionary,* s.v. "autonomous morality", 49; see also Ben Coburn, *Autonomy and Liberalism,* Routledge Studies in Contemporary Philosophy 19 (New York: Routledge, 2010), 19: "Autonomy is an ideal of individuals deciding for themselves what is a valuable life and living their lives in accordance with that decision."

[51] Pius XII, Address to Participants in the VIII Congress of the World Medical Association (September 30, 1954).

[52] May, *Catholic Bioethics and the Gift of Human Life,* 247.

a temptation to live in a state of "interior revolt against the fact that one is a man"[53] (see QQ. 77–78) subject to God and the moral law.

69. Is the prevailing view of autonomy consistent with the Catholic Church's teaching regarding autonomy and human dignity?

No, the present-day tendency to view autonomy as each person's right to determine one's own moral values and apply them to one's own decisions is contrary to the Church's authoritative teaching. It purports to "create values", incorrectly alleges a "conflict between freedom and law", and elevates a person's opinion in the place of the "primacy of truth".[54] The modern view amounts to a claim of "absolute sovereignty"[55] by the person who asserts it, and "in effect deifies each person's free will".[56]

The Catholic Church has a rich history of teaching that God has endowed man with free will and conferred on him the dignity of a person.[57] "The dignity of the human person is rooted in his creation in the image and likeness of God" and "fulfilled in his vocation to divine beatitude."[58] An emphasis on the dignity of man has increasingly become how the Church seeks to communicate its traditional teaching on man's creation in the image of God to the modern world.[59]

[53] Jacques Maritain, *Moral Philosophy: An Historical and Critical Survey of the Great Systems* (New York: Scribner, 1964), 454.

[54] John Paul II, encyclical letter *Veritatis splendor* (The Splendor of the Truth) (August 6, 1993), no. 35.

[55] John Paul II, *Veritatis splendor*, no. 35; see also no. 40.

[56] Hardon, *Modern Catholic Dictionary*, s.v. "autonomous morality", 49.

[57] See *Catechism of the Catholic Church*, no. 1730.

[58] *Catechism of the Catholic Church*, no. 1700.

[59] Marc D. Guerra, "The Affirmation of Genuine Human Dignity", *Journal of Markets and Morality* 4, no. 2 (Fall 2001): 295, https://digitalcommons.assumption.edu/cgi/viewcontent.cgi?article=1006&context=theology-faculty.

Human dignity should not be understood as requiring the radical modern view of autonomy. To embrace the contemporary idea of autonomy—that is, that a person is bound only by the law he creates within himself—would require rejecting the divinely created moral order.[60] Legitimate freedom and autonomy, or self-legislation, are rooted in our creation in the image of God and must be guided by truth. Thus, man does not have the authority to create the laws by which he lives. The moral law comes from outside man—from God himself. "Man's *genuine moral autonomy* in no way means the rejection but rather the acceptance of the moral law, of God's command: 'And the LORD God commanded the man' (Gen 2:16). *Human freedom and God's law meet and are called to intersect,* in the sense of man's free obedience to God and of God's completely gratuitous benevolence towards man."[61]

70. Is there a legitimate role of autonomy in end-of-life decisions?

Yes, but human autonomy and freedom are not unlimited. They must be guided by truth, and the truth ultimately comes from God and the moral law. As Saint Paul expressed, we are not our own: "None of us lives to himself, and none of us dies to himself. If we live, we live to the Lord, and if we die, we die to the Lord; so then, whether we live or whether we die, we are the Lord's. For to this end Christ died and lived again, that he might be Lord both of the dead and of the living" (Rom 14:7–9).

The value of our autonomy and freedom at the end of life comes from our ability to apply God's truth to the

[60] Guerra, "The Affirmation of Genuine Human Dignity", 299.
[61] John Paul II, *Veritatis splendor*, no. 41.

concrete facts of our circumstances of our own individual situations and to make wise and morally right choices that lead to our happiness and flourishing.

There are several end-of-life decisions where legitimate freedom and autonomy exist, guided by reason and the moral law. Well-reasoned choices and decisions are necessary. The Church respects competent adult patients' free and informed judgments concerning those choices, provided the decisions are not contrary to Catholic moral teaching.

71. Isn't a person free to seek a "death with dignity"?

Only insofar as a death with dignity is understood correctly. The phrase "death with dignity" needs careful definition and qualification because it has become a popular term for physician-assisted suicide and euthanasia. Because of the prevalent understanding of the phrase as used in modern society, a Christian should refrain from using the term.

No outward circumstances can remove a person's true dignity (see Q. 69), because this dignity comes from his very nature as made in God's image. However, the manner in which one dies should reflect this dignity. For example, it is a blessing for a Catholic to die at home, surrounded by family and friends, with time to express love and affection for them, confess his sins, and receive the anointing of the sick and Holy Communion (called viaticum—"food for the journey"—when received for the last time).

But this understanding of the ideal circumstances for death is decidedly *not* what the secular culture means when it uses the phrase "death with dignity". Instead, the phrase is often used as a euphemism for premature death, sometimes with the assistance of another person, and usually because the dying person is presumed to have a life not worth living or because society has declared that the life of the dying is a "burden". Thus, ironically, the phrase "death with dignity" is used precisely to deny the true dignity of the dying person.

V

HOW GOD SEES US AND THE SIGNIFICANCE OF THIS VISION FOR END-OF-LIFE DECISIONS

72. What does the Church teach about the gift of human life?

The Catholic Church teaches that "*human life is sacred* . . . and it remains for ever in a special relationship with the Creator, who is its sole end. God alone is the Lord of life from its beginning until its end: no one can under any circumstance claim for himself the right directly to destroy an innocent human being."[1] The Church's teaching regarding the value of human life is built upon the fifth commandment: "You shall not kill."

The gift of human life comes with a call to a fullness of life in God, which is much greater than our earthly existence.[2] As Pope John Paul II writes, "Life on earth is not an 'ultimate' but a 'penultimate' reality; even so, it remains a sacred reality entrusted to us, to be preserved with a sense of responsibility and brought to perfection in love and in the gift of ourselves to God and to our brothers and sisters."[3]

73. What is the prevailing attitude toward human life in this age?

In this modern age, we are facing an "extraordinary increase and gravity of threats"[4] to the lives of all people, especially those entering the world and those leaving it for eternity. The predominant tendency today is to value life

[1] *Catechism of the Catholic Church*, no. 2258 (emphasis in original).

[2] John Paul II, encyclical letter *Evangelium vitae* (The Gospel of Life) (March 25, 1995), no. 2.

[3] John Paul II, *Evangelium vitae*, no. 2.

[4] John Paul II, *Evangelium vitae*, nos. 3, 44.

only to the extent that it brings pleasure and well-being and to see suffering as "senseless".[5]

The Church and the Word of God call for special care and respect where life is undermined by sickness and old age.[6] Thus, end-of-life care and decision-making are of critical importance in a world with increasing threats to the dignity and existence of man.

74. What is a man and what is he like?

God made man an image of himself, with a mind and free will, and he has two essential aspects—a material body and a spiritual soul[7] (see Q. 35). The body and soul form one substance in this life, but they separate at death. Man's soul, being immaterial and spiritual, is immortal. His soul thus lives forever, but his earthly body does not, and the decisions man makes in this life can determine where he will spend eternity.

The *Catechism* tells us that since man is created in the image of God, he "possesses the dignity of a person, who is not just something, but someone. He is capable of self-knowledge, of self-possession and of freely giving himself and entering into communion with other persons. And he is called by grace to a covenant with his Creator, to offer him a response of faith and love that no other creature can give in his stead."[8]

[5] John Paul II, *Evangelium vitae*, no. 64.

[6] John Paul II, *Evangelium vitae*, no. 44.

[7] This is the Church's constant teaching from Holy Scripture and the Church Fathers, confirmed in councils, particularly the Fourth Lateran Council and Vatican Council I, regarding the two essential aspects of man. See especially *Catechism of the Catholic Church*, no. 357 and no. 363: the soul is "the innermost aspect of man, that which is of greatest value to him, that by which he is most especially in God's image". The soul is the source of all of man's activities, and its two highest powers are the intellect, by which he knows things, and the will, by which he decides and acts.

[8] *Catechism of the Catholic Church*, no. 357.

In this age, especially in the context of advances in medical treatments and technologies, it is critical to keep in mind that the inherent dignity and intrinsic value of every human being never change, "no matter what the concrete circumstances of his or her life".[9] Whether severely ill or nearing death, every person possesses a person's dignity and remains someone.

75. What duties do all men owe God?

Man's primary duty is to obtain his ultimate and final end: to glorify God and enjoy eternal happiness with him. Man's specific duties are to know, hope in, love, and worship the one true God.[10] Man's knowledge of God is attained by reason (through the natural law inscribed in his heart) and revelation (Sacred Scriptures and Sacred Tradition). To guide us in these duties, the Church's Magisterium *gives the authentic interpretation of revelation.*[11]

76. What are my duties to God in end-of-life matters?

[9] Pope John Paul II, "Life-Sustaining Treatments and Vegetative State" (March 20, 2004), no. 3.

[10] See *Catechism of the Catholic Church*, nos. 1–3.

[11] Divine revelation was initially handed down by word of mouth. Eventually, it was committed to writing. Both means of transmission were provided under the infallible inspiration of the Holy Spirit. Revelation handed down orally is known as Sacred Tradition, and revelation committed to writing is known as Sacred Scripture (the Bible). Sacred Tradition and Scripture form one sacred deposit of faith—the Word of God. The authentic interpretation of the deposit of faith (the Word of God), whether in oral or written form, is entrusted to the Church's Magisterium. See First Vatican Council, First Dogmatic Constitution on the Church of Christ *Pastor aeternus* (July 18, 1870), chapter IV, https://www.ewtn.com/catholicism/teachings/vatican-is -dogmatic-constitution-pastor-aeternus-on-the-church-of-christ-243: "For the Holy Spirit was promised to the successors of Peter not so that they might, by his revelation, make known some new doctrine, but that, by his assistance they might religiously guard and faithfully expound the revelation or deposit of faith transmitted by the apostles."

We are ordered toward happiness in truth, so we are bound to seek the truth in all things, especially things that concern God and his Church, "and to embrace it and hold on to it as [we] come to know it".[12]

In matters of life, particularly end-of-life decisions, we must keep in mind that "we are not the owners of our lives, and, hence, do not have absolute power over life. We have a duty to preserve our life and to use it for the glory of God."[13] This duty is not absolute in end-of-life situations, but it precludes any actions contrary to the moral law.

These duties together make it clear that we have a responsibility to God to seek truth in matters that pertain to God and the Church's teachings, especially relating to preserving our life and using it for God's glory.

There is also a duty to care for oneself. The Church teaches, "Certainly there is a moral obligation to care for oneself and to allow oneself to be cared for, but this duty must take account of concrete circumstances."[14] This is discussed in greater detail in Q. 11, but concrete circumstances may include a variety of things, such as one's age, current medical condition, the prognosis for recovery, family status and duties to dependents, the burden and benefits of specific medical treatments, whether one maintains the status quo or forgoes or accepts a medical intervention, and the financial impact on oneself and one's family.

Given the increasing threats to life at its most vulnerable stages, what is known as the "culture of death" twists terms such as "cost", "burden", and "quality of life" to hasten the death of a loved one. It is essential to understand the

[12] *Catechism of the Catholic Church*, no. 2104 (quoting Vatican Council II, Declaration on Religious Freedom *Dignitatis humanae* [December 7, 1965], no. 1).
[13] United States Conference of Catholic Bishops, *Ethical and Religious Directives for Catholic Health Care Services*, part five, introduction.
[14] John Paul II, *Evangelium vitae*, 65.

proper parameters of those terms. Appropriately understood, a matter such as cost (see QQ. 27–28), burden (QQ.
12–13, 27–28), or quality of life (QQ. 56–58) may be *a* factor but never the *sole* factor in end-of-life decision-making.
The duty to care for oneself, a fundamental commitment,
does not change when one is in the hospital.

Finally, physicians, nurses, and other caregivers, especially Catholic caregivers, have an essential duty to care
for others (their neighbors), especially those at the end of
life.[15]

77. What is the "human condition"?

The Christian faith teaches that man was created good,
without sin, suffering, and death. From this state, the first
man (Adam) fell through his own fault, by disobeying the
will of God. As a result, all his descendants were born separated from God and with a tendency to resist him. In the
fullness of time, the Son of God became man to repair the
broken relationship between God and his children through
his perfect obedience unto death. He rose from the dead,
returned to the Father, and sent his Spirit, so that man, by
uniting himself to Christ, can be regenerated into an obe-
dient son of God and supernaturally transfigured in Christ
at the end of history as we know it.

The human condition is such that man lives in a "vale
of tears", but he is destined for everlasting life with God.
Man must make his way to heaven amid a world filled
with evil, suffering, and death. By enduring these very
things, his love is purified, and he attains the ultimate happiness he seeks.

---

[15] Congregation for the Doctrine of the Faith, *Letter "Samaritanus bonus" of
the Congregation for the Doctrine of the Faith on the Care of Persons in the Critical and
Terminal Phases of Life* (September 22, 2020), section I.

78. What does the human condition have to do with end-of-life decisions?

Man is naturally tempted to deny his true condition in this life. As Jacques Maritain observes, it is possible to live in a state of "interior revolt against the fact that one is a man".[16] This is particularly tempting when one is faced with aging and with impending death.

In end-of-life decisions, this temptation can be manifest by an overwhelming attraction toward technologies and medical interventions that help us avoid or minimize the human condition, particularly suffering and the possibility of burdensome illness or a difficult death. A denial of the human condition can also lead us to recoil at any obstacle to earthly happiness or to grasp for anything that purports to give us power over our human nature. As one might presume, these effects can make prudent decisions challenging to attain at the end of life.

It is not wrong or unnatural to want to avoid losing legitimate autonomy as we age or to minimize pain and suffering (see QQ. 68–70). Still, in doing so, we must be on guard against the temptation to live in a state of internal revolt against the fact that we are only human. We must see ourselves as God sees us and trust in his loving care.

79. Are we merely to accept our human condition and resign ourselves to this "vale of tears"?

No. We should neither resign ourselves to our human condition nor deny the reality of it. Instead, we should strive to transform it. God made man for happiness, so we have a natural desire to be happy. As good as God's

---

[16]Jacques Maritain, *Moral Philosophy: An Historical and Critical Survey of the Great Systems* (New York: Scribner, 1964), 454.

creation is in itself, because of the Fall, this world is currently a vale of tears, meaning there are contradictions, sin, suffering, and death. But human beings can act for an end—the end of happiness, which ultimately consists of life in God. This can be done regardless of man's condition and the difficulties of this life.

Our lives on earth are more or less happy depending on our choices, and good choices can move us farther toward everlasting happiness. In the context of end-of-life decisions, the more aware we are of the tendency to deny our human condition inappropriately, the better able we are to make good end-of-life choices.

VI

HAPPINESS AND ITS RELATION
TO MORAL DECISION-MAKING

80. What do human beings desire and seek more than anything else?

A human being has many desires, some of which even conflict with others. Some people seek pleasure, fame, or fortune, while others seek only to get by and have a comfortable life. But one desire above all others gives meaning to all the endless desires a man has over his life. That desire is happiness.

Happiness is the goal of all human activity, and it is the goal all human beings seek when they make choices.[1] The person who intensely desires and decides to buy a beautiful automobile is not seeking a car; he is seeking happiness, which he believes the automobile will bring. The man prospecting for gold does not seek gold; he seeks the happiness he thinks gold will bring.

The desire for happiness is the common ground of all human acts and choices, but since man is made in the image of God, his happiness cannot ultimately be found in wealth, power, or fame.[2] Man's ultimate happiness cannot even be found in his health or any bodily good.[3]

81. What does a person's desire for happiness have to do with end-of-life decision-making?

[1] See Thomas Aquinas, *Summa Theologiae*, II-I, q. 1, a. 8.
[2] Thomas Aquinas, *Summa Theologiae*, II-I, q. 3, a. 1-4; see also Peter E. Bristow, *The Moral Dignity of Man* (Dublin, Ireland: Four Courts Press, 1997), 36; the author notes that, given man's creation in the image of God, he is ordered toward ultimate happiness in truth, which as St. Thomas Aquinas said, all men know to be God.
[3] Thomas Aquinas, *Summa Theologiae*, II-I, q. 3, a. 5.

Simply put, God has created us in such a way that we naturally desire happiness, and we more or less achieve that happiness through our practical decisions. Nowhere is that more important than in the way we age and prepare for death.

Since man is designed to desire happiness, he naturally seeks happiness in his decisions and choices. This is true even though he may not know in what happiness consists.[4] This can easily occur in the context of end-of-life decisions. For example, a person who decides in favor of an immoral medical intervention to avoid suffering seeks happiness when he does so, even though he does not understand that his decision will not attain him true happiness.

82. Where is a person's ultimate happiness to be found?

Final and perfect happiness can be found in God alone.[5] This is the only object in which every person's desire can find rest and, as Saint Augustine observes, we are restless until we find our rest in God. God has made us so that we tend toward him with our whole being. This tendency toward God is a deep-seated impulse within us so that every action we perform in accordance with our nature is toward the end for which we have been created—toward communion with God.[6]

Thus, man's ultimate happiness (his highest good) is not to preserve his life forever on earth or even to avoid pain and suffering. It is in the communion of love face-to-face with Christ.

[4] Thomas J. Higgins, S.J., *Man as Man: The Science and Art of Ethics* (Rockford, IL: Tan Books, 1958), 18–19.

[5] Thomas Aquinas, *Summa Theologiae*, II-I, q. 3, a. 8, 601.

[6] Charles Coppens, S.J., *A Brief Text-book of Moral Philosophy*, ed. Paul A. Böer, Sr. (Edmond, OK: Veritatis Splendor Publications, 2012), 13.

83. How do we attain ultimate happiness?

By revelation, we know that God, by his goodness and wisdom, has made known to man the way to eternal happiness. He "'desires all men to be saved and to come to the knowledge of the truth' that is, of Christ Jesus".[7] In short, God wants all men and women everywhere to make their way to Heaven and enjoy the communion of love face-to-face with Christ. "Final and perfect happiness can consist in nothing else than the vision of Divine Essence [of God]."[8]

84. What does the morality of practical decisions have to do with our ultimate happiness?

Man is a body and soul unity, created in the image of God. All his acts are moral acts in the sense that, if they are done consciously and freely, they either lead him nearer to his ultimate end and supreme happiness (life with God), or they lead him farther away from it.[9] So, given human nature, a person will inevitably be faced with decisions on end-of-life issues that have moral consequences.

Pope John Paul II, in his encyclical *Veritatis splendor*, notes that "the moral life has an essential '*teleological*' character" because a person deliberately orders his acts to God (his ultimate end), and a Christian "by his actions ... lives out his fidelity or infidelity ... and he opens or closes himself to eternal life" by those actions.[10]

If a person makes a morally good end-of-life decision, he will move nearer to his eternal happiness (by living out his fidelity and opening himself to eternal life); if he makes a morally bad end-of-life decision, he will move farther

---

[7] *Catechism of the Catholic Church*, no. 74 (quoting 1 Tim 2:4 and Jn 14:6).

[8] Thomas Aquinas, *Summa Theologiae*, II-I, q. 3, a. 8, 601.

[9] Bristow, *The Moral Dignity of Man*, 34.

[10] John Paul II, encyclical letter *Veritatis splendor* (The Splendor of the Truth) (August 6, 1993), no. 73.

away from his supreme happiness (by living out his infidelity and closing himself to eternal life).

85. How should we relate our practical moral decisions to our ultimate happiness in God?

Since our ultimate end is happiness in God, our wills are directed by God to seek happiness, and we cannot rest until we find it. When we make a free and conscious practical decision about the right and wrong of end-of-life treatment, we are pursuing happiness. If our practical decision coincides objectively with reaching our ultimate happiness in God, we move closer to finding that happiness.

Thus, in making practical end-of-life decisions, we should never forget that our ultimate end is eternal happiness in God. However reasonable it may appear to focus on the more immediate goals of relieving pain and suffering, decreasing burden, or exercising personal freedom, such goals should not become ends in themselves. They should always be considered with the ultimate and eternal end in mind.

86. What is a good moral decision in relation to our happiness?

Man's will is naturally ordered toward happiness, and his ultimate end is everlasting happiness with God (see QQ. 87–88). A moral act or decision is thus one knowingly and freely made to achieve man's ultimate end. Pope John Paul II alluded to this when he wrote, "The *morality of acts* is defined by the relationship of man's freedom with the authentic good."[11] A practical decision that moves a person closer to his end of happiness in God is a good, moral decision. One that moves him farther away from his ultimate end is a bad, immoral decision.

[11] John Paul II, *Veritatis splendor*, no. 72.

VII

THE MORAL LAW AND MORAL
DECISION-MAKING

87. How do the moral categories of good and evil even apply in end-of-life decisions? Don't such decisions depend upon changing circumstances and the personal opinions of the patient or loved one?

No. The good or evil of an act or decision does not change with the circumstances or personal opinions of the actor. Circumstances can be important in determining a good or bad action (see Q. 11), but they are never the sole determination.

The worldview of the modern age has been described as a "dictatorship of relativism".[1] It is no exaggeration to say that most people do not see the moral categories of good and evil as objective. Instead, they view those categories as "corresponding to the different circumstances of the individual, and thus susceptible to change".[2] In short, the dominant modern view is that "good" and "evil" are relative terms that change depending on circumstances and subjective intentions.

The Catholic Church's constant and consistent teaching is that subjectivism and relativism in morality are to be rejected. The categories of good and evil are objective, not simply a matter of opinion or circumstances. An act of murder remains a murder even when called by another name—like euthanasia, mercy killing, or medical aid in dying.

[1] Joseph Cardinal Ratzinger, Homily, Vatican Basilica, April 18, 2005, https://www.vatican.va/gpII/documents/homily-pro-eligendo-pontifice_20050418_en.html.

[2] Aurelio Fernández and James Socías, *Our Moral Life in Christ: A Basic Course on Moral Theology* (Princeton, NJ: Scepter Publishers, 1997), 110.

88. Is there an objective guide to help ensure that our end-of-life decisions are morally good?

Yes. Despite the inclination by many to believe all principles and norms for human conduct come from everyone's autonomous will (see QQ. 68–69), the moral law is the objective norm of all human conduct. It is a rule of conduct enacted by God for our good to help us achieve our ultimate end (see QQ. 83–86).

89. What is the moral law, and what is its relationship to decision-making at the end of life?

The moral law is the norm for human conduct, "whether revealed or known by reason".[3] It is thus the standard for making good moral decisions, but it is not a list of "dos and don'ts". On the contrary, it is better understood as "fatherly instruction" that leads us to happiness (see Part VI).[4] The moral law has different expressions (e.g., revealed and natural), but these expressions form one unified law.[5]

The moral law provides the rule for human conduct and moral decision-making at every stage of life, including

[3] John Hardon, *Modern Catholic Dictionary* (Garden City, NY: Doubleday, 1980), s.v. "Moral law", 360.

[4] The *Catechism of the Catholic Church*, no. 1950, describes it as "the work of divine Wisdom. Its biblical meaning can be defined as fatherly instruction, God's pedagogy. It prescribes for man the ways, the rules of conduct that lead to the promised beatitude; it proscribes the ways of evil which turn him away from God and his love. It is at once firm in its precepts and, in its promises, worthy of love."

[5] *Catechism of the Catholic Church*, no. 1952. Some theologians use different terms (other than "moral law") to express the standards that determine the moral character of human acts. For example, the great moral theologian Dominic M. Prümmer, O.P., *Handbook of Moral Theology*, trans. Gerald W. Shelton (Manchester, NH: Benedictus Books, 2022), includes under the heading "Divine Law" the eternal law, natural law, and divine positive law, which includes the Holy Scripture.

the end of life. In summary, it specifies for man the way and rules of conduct that lead to God and prohibits the evil acts and behavior that "turn him away from God and his love".[6]

90. What is the moral law that can be known by reason?

The moral law known by reason is called the natural law. The natural law is "nothing else than the rational creature's participation in the eternal law".[7] A way of understanding this is that the natural law is an expression of God's will, implanted in each man's heart and recognized by the natural light of reason. It is universal in its authoritative guidelines and communicates two things to everyone: (1) the primary and unchangeable principles of God's creation and (2) the immediate deductions from those principles—for example, the Ten Commandments.

These two things God communicates form a shared moral sense, as substantial as math and science, that human beings cannot not know.[8] From God's created order, for instance, a person cannot avoid his internal sense that there is something sacred about human life. From this principle, that person can deduce that it is wrong to murder a human being (the fifth commandment). A human being cannot *not* know these things. There does not need to be a positive law to state a common-sense moral truth—all men possess this natural law. Unfortunately, a person can suppress, and even lie to himself about, what he knows,

---

[6] *Catechism of the Catholic Church*, no. 1950.

[7] Thomas Aquinas, *Summa Theologiae*, I-II, q. 91, a. 2. A simple way of understanding the eternal law is God's wise plan for all creation that is directed from eternity and ordered toward the universe's good.

[8] J. Budziszewski, *What We Can't Not Know: A Guide* (Dallas, TX: Spence Publishing, 2003), 19–21.

but he cannot entirely escape the truth of the natural law, because it is implanted in his heart (see Rom 1:19–21).

As it relates to decision-making, the natural law is what is known, or can be known, by human beings through the exercise of reason regarding God's creation and the things that clearly follow from that creation. In simple terms, the natural law is the eternal law written on every person's heart from birth, giving him a sense of fundamental right and wrong.[9]

91. What is the moral law that comes from revelation?

The revealed law is positive divine law, meaning all the prescriptions that God has given by supernatural revelation, distinct from the knowledge of God's will that the exercise of reason alone can attain.[10] The revealed law comprises the Holy Scripture (Old Testament, New Testament, and the Law of Christ).[11]

One may reasonably ask why the teachings of the Holy Scripture (revelation) are necessary as a moral guide if every person has the natural law implanted in his heart. The answer is that while the general universal principles of the natural law are embedded in all men, the secondary deductions from those principles can be obscured by sinful attractions, bad habits, evil passions, and even poor moral formation. Supernatural revelation is therefore needed to overcome the weakness of men, to make God's divine moral will perfectly clear, and to lead man to his eternal destiny.[12]

[9] Thomas Aquinas, *Summa Theologiae*, I-II, q. 91, a. 2: natural law "is nothing other than the rational creature's participation in the eternal law". By "natural", St. Thomas means rationally grasped or understood—through the exercise of reason.

[10] Hardon, *Modern Catholic Dictionary*, s.v. "revealed law", 467.

[11] See *Catechism of the Catholic Church*, no. 1952.

[12] See *Catechism of the Catholic Church*, no. 1960.

For example, the general principles of the natural law interiorly inform a person that human life is sacred and, consequently, one must not take one's own life. This cannot *not* be known. But physical suffering and psychological fears may obscure this principle, and poor moral formation may make the truth less distinct. Revelation, however, makes known "with a firm certainty and with freedom from all error"[13] that taking one's own life is always wrong and, depending on the circumstances, may be blameworthy as murder.

92. Is the moral law too complicated to be a helpful guide to making moral decisions at the end of life?

No. Recognizing and applying the moral law to concrete circumstances is not as complex as it might appear. The Church's Magisterium gives the authentic interpretation of the whole deposit of faith, including the moral law.[14] On numerous occasions, the Magisterium has provided specific guidance on the issues we address in this book, including but not limited to the following: the *Declaration on Euthanasia* by the Congregation for the Doctrine of the Faith (May 5, 1980), which addresses new questions posed by advances in medical technology; the instruction *Donum vitae* from the Congregation for the Doctrine of the Faith (February 22, 1987), which considers questions raised by bioethical technology; the encyclical *Veritatis splendor* (August 6, 1993), which responds to the crisis in Christian moral theology in the aftermath of the Second Vatican Council; the encyclical *Evangelium vitae* (March 25, 1995), which defends human life by denouncing the

[13] Pius XII, encyclical letter *Humani generis* (On the Unity of the Human Race) (August 12, 1950), no. 3.
[14] See *Catechism of the Catholic Church*, nos. 85–86.

dangers of a "culture of death" and condemning abortion, euthanasia, and suicide; and the letter *Samaritanus bonus* from the Congregation for the Doctrine of the Faith (July 14, 2020), which addresses the care of persons in the critical and terminal phases of life.

The Church's Magisterium, exercising its authority in the name of Jesus Christ, teaches what has been passed on to it and provides us with the guidance we need to deal with complicated end-of-life decisions and make our way to heaven. For moral decision-making and the purposes of this book, it is thus essential to know what the moral law teaches about human life, the ultimate end of man, human acts, and moral choices.

93. What issues arise at the end of life requiring choices between morally good and bad decisions?

Given the rapid rate of medical progress and developments in the last several decades, there are often complex issues facing persons at the end of life. The Catholic Church welcomes those developments and medical advancements, provided they are not intrinsically evil and are applied in a way that is consistent with the moral law. Unfortunately, some modern medical interventions are evil, and some are being used in a way that is contrary to the moral law.

Ordinary circumstances that arise requiring end-of-life decisions include questions such as the following: whether specific surgical procedures are appropriate; when death occurs (when the soul leaves the body) so that vital organs may be harvested; what constitutes irreversible terminal illness; whether physician-assisted euthanasia/suicide is ever permissible; whether life-support measures are appropriate and, if so, under what circumstances; whether drugs may be used to suppress pain and control suffering and, if so, how much, when, and under what circumstances; whether an advance directive is appropriate; and whether a DNR ("do not resuscitate") order is ever justified. These are not simple issues in themselves, and they are often made more complex by the concrete circumstances of individual persons. But they are increasingly familiar to people of advancing years.

94. What is moral reasoning?

Moral reasoning is using practical reason to understand and apply the correct moral principles to specific concrete circumstances in order to reach a proper decision about right and wrong.

95. What are some examples of end-of-life decisions that raise moral issues?

Perhaps identifying and understanding these decisions will be aided by comparing end-of-life issues with teaching on life issues better understood by Catholics, like issues involving the unborn child.

Once it is understood that embryology establishes the humanity of the unborn child from the moment of sperm-egg fusion (conception), it follows quickly that killing an innocent human being in the womb, at any stage of development, is always immoral. One must irrationally deny the undeniable to conclude otherwise. For similar reasons, it is relatively easy to understand that destructive human embryo research is always wrong. In both cases, it is uncomplicated to apply the moral law of the fifth commandment—"thou shall not kill"—to the concrete circumstances to distinguish right from wrong.

But end-of-life decision-making is not so straightforward. Is the removal or refusal of a ventilator an act of killing, or is it a morally acceptable act that simply allows the underlying disease to take its course? What about withholding artificial nutrition or hydration when death is imminent? Is the body shutting down and unable to assimilate food or water, or is the decision to withhold nutrition or hydration intentionally causing death by starvation and dehydration? Is the moral law (especially the fifth commandment) violated when certain types of medical therapies are discontinued or declined? If not, why not? The moral law is clear and knowable, but the decision in each one of these end-of-life contexts depends on critical components of moral choice and the concrete circumstances of the patient's condition.

96. What determines the morality of choice in any given action?

Human acts involve decisions about right and wrong. A human act is an act that is freely made with knowledge of the end or purpose in sight. This is to be distinguished from involuntary, merely instinctive, or accidental acts.[15]

The morality of any given action is determined by three factors: the object (QQ. 97–98), the intention (Q. 100), and the circumstances (Q. 101).[16] These elements are also called the three sources of the morality of human acts.[17]

The United States Conference of Catholic Bishops well summarizes these three elements: "Every moral act consists of three elements: the objective act (what we do), the subjective goal or intention (why we do the act), and

---

[15] See Henry Davis, S.J., *Moral and Pastoral Theology*, 8th ed., vols. 1 and 2 (New York: Sheed & Ward, 1959).

[16] Aurelio Fernández and James Socías, *Our Moral Life in Christ: A Basic Course on Moral Theology* (Princeton, NJ: Scepter Publishers, 1997), 106–9.

[17] See, e.g., *Catechism of the Catholic Church*, no. 1750.

the concrete situation or circumstances in which we perform the act (where, when, how, with whom, the consequences, etc.)."[18]

97. What is the "object" of a moral act?

In the physical order, the object is the act that is directly
willed and being done, such as walking, swimming, etc. In
the moral order (that is, matters of right and wrong), the
object is the act or decision a person objectively chooses.
Once an act or decision has occurred, the object often
becomes apparent to all. It is the state of affairs that is accomplished and that reason judges to be either good or evil.

One cannot do a moral act or make a morally good
decision unless what is being done is objectively good.
Pope John Paul II, citing Saint Thomas Aquinas, wrote,
"*The morality of the human act depends primarily and fundamentally on the 'object' rationally chosen by the deliberate will.*"[19]

In the context of end-of-life decision-making, a person
may not choose to do an act or make a decision about the
use of medical technology or choose a medical intervention that is objectively evil (e.g., depriving a seriously ill
patient of basic care; see QQ. 15–16).

98. Are there any objects in a moral act that are always wrong?

Yes. Certain objects are always morally wrong, "meaning
that they are wrong in themselves, apart from the reason

[18] "Morality", United States Conference of Catholic Bishops, excerpted
from *United States Catholic Catechism for Adults* (Washington, DC: United States
Catholic Conference of Bishops, 2006), accessed March 8, 2022, https://www
.usccb.org/beliefs-and-teachings/what-we-believe/morality.

[19] John Paul II, encyclical letter *Veritatis splendor* (The Splendor of the Truth)
(August 6, 1993), no. 78.

they are done or the circumstances surrounding them".[20] The *Catechism of the Catholic Church* refers to this when it states, "There are concrete acts that it is always wrong to choose, because their choice entails a disorder of the will, i.e., a moral evil."[21]

For example, murder is always a grave evil because of its object, which is intentionally to take the life of an innocent person. Blasphemy, rape, and adultery are other examples of grave evils because of the objects chosen by the person who acts. The actor directly chooses an objective wrong.[22]

99. Are there end-of-life decisions that are always wrong because the act chosen is a grave sin?

Yes. The Church often uses the term "intrinsic evil" to describe certain kinds of human acts that can never be morally justified, regardless of intention (see Q. 98). The *Catechism of the Catholic Church* states: "There are acts, which, in and of themselves, independently of circumstances and intentions, are always gravely illicit by reason of their object; such as blasphemy and perjury, murder and adultery."[23] Examples of intrinsically evil objects in an end-of-life context are euthanasia, suicide, and assisted

[20] "Morality", United States Conference of Catholic Bishops, excerpted from *United States Catholic Catechism for Adults* (Washington, DC: United States Catholic Conference of Bishops, 2006), accessed March 8, 2022, https://www.usccb.org/beliefs-and-teachings/what-we-believe/morality.

[21] *Catechism of the Catholic Church*, no. 1761.

[22] See Henry Davis, S.J., *Moral and Pastoral Theology*, 8th ed. (New York: Sheed & Ward, 1959), 1:55; see also the *Catechism of the Catholic Church*, no. 1755: "The *object of the choice* can by itself vitiate an act in its entirety. There are some concrete acts—such as fornication—that it is always wrong to choose, because choosing them entails a disorder of the will, that is, a moral evil" (emphasis in original).

[23] *Catechism of the Catholic Church*, no. 1756.

suicide.[24] Under no set of circumstances may a Catholic choose these acts. Depending on the circumstances, it is possible for euthanasia to constitute suicide or murder.[25] Furthermore, the Church teaches that "*any formal or immediate material cooperation* in such an act is a grave sin against human life."[26]

100. What is the "intention" of a moral act?

The intention is the reason for acting. It answers the question, "Why am I doing this?" For a decision or act to be moral, not only must there be an objectively good object, but a person must do nothing contrary to right reason and have a good intention that is related to God, at least implicitly. He cannot accomplish a moral act by intending to act for pleasure alone.[27]

The morality of a human act comes primarily from the objective object. It must be good, but it is not enough for the object to be good; it must also be intended as a good. If the object is good, but the intention is bad, it spoils the good act and renders it morally bad.[28]

---

[24] Congregation for the Doctrine of the Faith, *Letter "Samaritanus bonus" of the Congregation for the Doctrine of the Faith on the Care of Persons in the Critical and Terminal Phases of Life* (September 22, 2020), section 1; see also John Paul II, *Evangelium vitae*, no. 66.

[25] Congregation for the Doctrine of the Faith, *Samaritanus bonus*, section 1.

[26] Congregation for the Doctrine of the Faith, *Samaritanus bonus*, section 1 (emphasis in original). It is beyond the scope of this book to discuss "formal or immediate material cooperation" in intrinsically evil acts, as the concept applies primarily to health-care workers in the contemporary health-care context of abortion, euthanasia, assisted suicide, and direct sterilization. We encourage those interested in this topic, particularly health-care workers, to begin by reading the summary prepared by National Catholic Bioethics Center ethicists: "Cooperation with Moral Evil", which is available on the NCBC's website.

[27] See Dominic M. Prümmer, O.P., *Handbook of Moral Theology*, trans. Gerald W. Shelton (Manchester, NH: Benedictus Books, 2022), 27–28.

[28] Henry Davis, S.J., *Moral and Pastoral Theology*, 8th ed. (New York: Sheed & Ward, 1959), 1:59.

It is also essential to remember that a good intention cannot make an intrinsically evil act good.[29] For example, a person cannot make the intrinsic evil of assisted suicide good by an intention to be merciful (that is, to relieve pain and suffering). A compassionate intention cannot decontaminate an intrinsically evil behavior. [30]

101. What are the "circumstances" of a moral act?

The circumstances of an act are the concrete conditions or situations that surround and concur with an action. They may be determined through a series of questions: Who? What? Where? Why? How? and When? The *Catechism* explains: "The *circumstances*, including the consequences, are secondary elements of a moral act. They contribute to increasing or diminishing the moral goodness or evil of human acts (for example, the amount of a theft). They can also diminish or increase the agent's responsibility (such as acting out of a fear of death). Circumstances of themselves cannot change the moral quality of acts themselves; they can make neither good nor right an action that is in itself evil."[31]

The Church's teachings on the moral law and the principles respecting the dignity of human life are well developed. But what is confusing to many is the application of the principles to concrete facts in what may be the unique circumstances of a specific patient with a particular medical condition. Since illness and death of all persons will differ according to the circumstances accompanying disease and death, no universal formula or algorithm exists

---

[29] *Catechism of the Catholic Church*, no. 1753: "The end does not justify the means."

[30] See *Catechism of the Catholic Church*, no. 1753.

[31] *Catechism of the Catholic Church*, no. 1754 (emphasis in original).

to guarantee easy end-of-life moral decisions. Decisions at the end of life are often made in a moment of medical crisis, emotional distress, and limited understanding of the disease and the options for its treatment.

What is needed is a firm grasp of the Church's end-of-life teaching, rooted in the natural law, Holy Scripture, and Tradition. It is also necessary to understand the ultimate end of man and to embrace the truth of the Church's teaching that our highest good is not to preserve life on earth or to avoid suffering. It is to find our ultimate happiness in truth—the communion of love face-to-face with Christ.

VIII

PREPARING AND PLANNING FOR SERIOUS ILLNESS AND THE END OF LIFE

102. If the soul takes priority over the body, what should I do to prepare it for serious illness and the end of life?

Simply put, one must learn to practice the *ars moriendi*—the art of dying. In reality, however, the art of dying is about much more than the hour of our death. It is about living one's life in a way that leads to happiness and prepares one for a good end. This is what Saint Robert Bellarmine meant when he wrote, "This first great truth now remains established: a good death depends upon a good life."[1] Bellarmine makes clear that this is an art that must be learned, and he can envision no greater folly than to neglect that art, "on which depend our highest and eternal interests".[2]

It is a mistake to see the art of dying as some morbid and outdated approach to preparing for illness and death. The wisdom of living well and dying well—of pursuing ultimate happiness—comes from centuries of Catholic teaching and culture. And never has it been more relevant than today, when threats to living faithfully and dying well have become so significant.

In the excellent introduction to *The Art of Dying: A New Annotated Translation*,[3] translator and Dominican physician

---

[1] Robert Bellarmine, *The Art of Dying Well: Or, How to Be a Saint, Now and Forever* (Manchester, NH: Sophia Institute Press, 2021), 5.

[2] See Robert Bellarmine, *The Art of Dying Well* (London: Richardson and Son, 1847), preface.

[3] *The Art of Dying: A New Annotated Translation*, trans. Columba Thomas (Philadelphia: The National Catholic Bioethics Center, 2021).

Brother Columba Thomas notes that contemporary bio-ethicists have looked to the medieval *ars moriendi* for inspiration in developing approaches to the end of life.[4] One such author is Dr. L. S. Dugdale, in her *The Lost Art of Dying: Reviving Forgotten Wisdom*.[5] It is not a religious book, but it builds upon a Christian foundation and captures well the fact that preparation for severe illness and death must be made in advance. Unfortunately, as Dugdale's subtitle indicates, this is "forgotten wisdom" that must be regained and practiced.

103. Are there principles to guide me or practical steps to take now to begin to practice the *ars moriendi*?

Yes. The following simple suggestions help prepare for aging, serious illness, and dying. These are presented in greater detail in Appendix III, which includes some excellent resources for deepening the spiritual life and preparing for serious illness and death.

We must acknowledge our mortality. It is impossible to make moral decisions at the end of life or ultimately to die well without coming to grips with the fact that we will die. This may strike one as self-evident, but an inability to acknowledge our mortality, except in the abstract, often leads to unrealistic expectations of recovery from severe illness and a "survive at all costs" mentality. This makes reasonable decisions and appropriate preparations at the end of life virtually impossible. We need to embrace the fact of our finite earthly existence and be able to discuss it openly and candidly.

---

[4] See *The Art of Dying: A New Annotated Translation*, 3.

[5] Dugdale's thoughtful work is founded upon significant research and experience as a medical ethicist and primary-care doctor.

We must understand that the soul is a higher priority than the body. Steps should be taken to understand and meditate on this essential principle for making moral decisions at the end of life and in the art of dying. This necessity is highlighted in the *Ars moriendi* and well explained in the introduction to *The Art of Dying: A New Annotated Translation.* Brother Columba Thomas explains why the *Ars moriendi* emphasizes recognizing and responding to the spiritual temptations that come when death approaches. The reason for these temptations is that the soul is a higher priority than the body, and "the tremendous worth of the soul motivates the devil to afflict the dying with the 'greatest temptations' to bring about their 'eternal death'; in other words, the devil himself understands the priority of the soul over the body and is thus primarily concerned with the death of the soul."[6] Failure to understand this crucial principle may leave a person unprepared to deal with the spiritual temptations that inevitably come with suffering and the approach of death.

We should begin the process of detaching ourselves from the things of this world. As Saint Robert Bellarmine noted, dying well requires living well. Preparations for facing severe illness and death must begin now while we are not beleaguered by disease and fully possess our reason. Bellarmine's *The Art of Dying Well* can be an invaluable aid in this process of detachment from the world and its possessions.

We should give appropriate attention to the things necessary for eternal life. The *Ars moriendi* provides a

[6] *The Art of Dying: A New Annotated Translation,* 7–8. The *Ars moriendi* spends significant time explaining that the dying face more serious temptations than ever before. It focuses on five such temptations and the good inspirations to counter those temptations.

succinct and well-known medieval summary of the things needed for the salvation of the one approaching death:

> First, he should believe as a faithful Christian does, and even rejoice, that he will die in the faith of Christ and the Church, united with them in obedience. Second, he should recognize that he has gravely offended God and grieve because of it. Third, he should resolve that if he recovers, he will amend his ways and never sin again. Fourth, he should forgive those who have offended him, for the sake of God, and ask forgiveness from those he has offended. Fifth, he should make restitution for the things he has taken. Sixth, he should know that Christ died for him and that there is no other way he can be saved except by the merit of the Passion of Christ, for which he should give thanks to God as much as possible. If he is able to assent to these items with a sincere heart, it is a sign that he is to be numbered among the saved.[7]

Pope John Paul II in *Evangelium vitae* generally alludes to things necessary as death approaches: "As they approach death people ought to be able to satisfy their moral and family duties, and above all they ought to be able to prepare in a fully conscious way for their definitive meeting with God."[8]

104. What does treating a patient with dignity mean at the end of life?

To be treated with dignity at the end of life means that after a long and fruitful life, facing imminent death, the dying person's moral treatment wishes are respected, the person is

---

[7] *The Art of Dying: A New Annotated Translation*, 38–39.

[8] John Paul II, encyclical letter *Evangelium vitae* (The Gospel of Life) (March 25, 1995), no. 65.

made comfortable (to the degree possible), and the person can attend to spiritual and family duties.

For a Catholic, being treated with dignity includes means to ensure that all health-care decisions are made in conformity with the Church's teaching and legal means are in place to ensure the guiding principles of decision-making are followed if one has an end-stage medical condition or is permanently unconscious.

If a Catholic falls terminally ill, treating him with dignity requires telling him about his condition without delay so that preparations for a holy death may be made. If the person cannot understand, communicate, or make decisions, a Catholic priest should be contacted to attend to the patient's spiritual needs.

105. What preparations can I make now to ease my anxiety about suffering at the end of my life?

Understanding and meditating on the deeper meaning of suffering can help diminish fear and anxiety. Graces are often concealed under the most improbable appearances, and nowhere more than the experience of suffering in illness and at the end of life. Serious illness is a test that can lead us to anguish, self-absorption, and even despair,[9] or it can lead to a deeper intimacy with Jesus Christ and a purifying conversion of life (see QQ 62–65). In Appendix III, we recommend two timeless works (*Self-Abandonment to Divine Providence* and *Trustful Surrender to Divine Providence*) that, if read and reflected upon, can help one begin to look at suffering from an entirely different perspective.

The Catholic faith teaches us that God's divine action upholds everything, encompasses everything, and directs

[9] See *Catechism of the Catholic Church*, nos. 1500–1502.

everything, apart from sin. It falls to us then, by faith, to love, welcome, and adore everything God sends our way—including suffering. In so doing, we discover a new dimension and receive a special grace to a sort of sanctity that draws us intimately close to Christ and into the deeper salvific meaning of suffering.[10]

Admittedly, it is not easy to reach the point of voluntarily welcoming suffering into our lives. That is one of the reasons advance preparations should be made before serious illness arrives. We recommend three means of helping to alleviate fear and anxiety by preparing to experience the deeper meaning of suffering if, and when, it comes: (1) reading and meditating on New Testament Scriptures on suffering, along with the short book *Trustful Surrender to Divine Providence* and the more detailed *Self-Abandonment to Divine Providence*; (2) practicing loving God and his plan in everything that comes our way by giving thanks, desiring nothing more; and (3) when suffering comes, abandoning ourselves to the present moment. "A holy soul is but a soul freely submitted to the divine will with the help of grace."[11]

106. What preparations can I make now to ease anxiety about the care I receive at the end of my life?

Careful instructions for future care can lessen fear and anxiety. Attention should be given to specific instructions for future care if an incurable and irreversible medical condition reaches an advanced state. Particularly, guidance

---

[10] See John Paul II, *Salvifici doloris* (On the Christian Meaning of Human Suffering) (February 11, 1984), no. 26.

[11] J. P. de Caussade, *Self-Abandonment to Divine Providence* (Rockford, IL: Tan Books, 1959), 55.

should be provided for attending to spiritual needs, exercising religious duties (to the degree possible) to prepare to meet God, creating an opportunity for a final expression of love for one's spouse and children (to the degree possible), and caring for one's mortal remains (see QQ. 119–23).

Instructions for health providers should include a presumption in favor of nutrition and hydration, including medically assisted nutrition and hydration, if they are capable of sustaining life and not causing harm. They should also include the presumption that any act or omission that, of itself, or by intention, directly causes death to eliminate suffering is not in accord with the moral law and the teachings of the Catholic faith. Clear guidance is needed regarding obligatory and basic care (food, water, and comfort) and optional treatments (therapies and interventions when death is imminent and inevitable that would be disproportionate to any expected results or would impose an excessive burden on the patient and his family given the concrete circumstances of his condition). (See QQ. 9–33.)

107. What kind of legal preparations can I make for the end of my life, and can any ensure that my end-of-life treatments are consistent with the Church's teachings?

Nothing in this book is intended as legal advice, and we encourage readers to seek legal counsel. Important legal preparations regarding care and treatment must be made ahead of a life-threatening hospitalization. The list of possible choices and legal documents can be intimidating, but it doesn't have to be. While not intended as legal advice, the following questions will examine a variety of legal documents that can be used in end-of-life decision-making, with brief explanatory comments:

advance directives in general (see Q. 108), medical power of attorney (see Q. 109), living wills (see Q. 110), physician orders for life-sustaining treatment (POLST) (see Q. 111), wills and trusts (see Q. 112), and HIPAA release (see Q. 113). We recommend medical power of attorney as the best legal means of ensuring that Catholic teachings are followed in end-of-life care decisions.

108. What is an advance directive, and what are the moral questions surrounding it?

In a book of this type, it is difficult to provide accurate information on legal documents applicable in all fifty states. As used in this book, the term "advance directives" refers to legal documents prepared in advance of a medical crisis that convey one's instructions about end-of-life care. We are not providing legal advice, and readers are encouraged to seek legal advice in their states on specific legal questions.

If written in terms consistent with the moral law and the Church's teachings, advance directives are not morally objectionable in principle.[12] Advance directives are, however, seldom drafted in this way. In the way they are usually written, they are morally objectionable because

[12] A good example of such an advance directive is The National Catholic Bioethics Center (NCBC) Health Care Proxy form that includes a page titled "Advance Medical Directive". Rather than specifying specific medical procedures to be declined or accepted based on unknown future facts, the one-page document gives general instructions to help the health-care agent make decisions on the patient's behalf. It includes language that instructs the agent to avoid authorizing anything that directly causes death (euthanasia) and clarifies that medical treatment can be refused or withdrawn if death is imminent and the treatment is one that only "maintain[s] a precarious and burdensome prolongation of my life". The NCBC form further includes blanks a Catholic may fill out ahead of time, indicating special provisions that the agent might consider given certain circumstances.

they prematurely decline specific medical care before a patient, his physician, loved ones, or health-care proxy has adequate knowledge of the concrete circumstances of his medical condition. In practice, this problem leads to declining specific medical care that is ordinary (such as food and water) or otherwise medically advisable given the circumstances.

If an advance directive is used, we recommend it be done in consultation with the National Catholic Bioethics Center (NCBC), which can be arranged through their website at https://www.ncbcenter.org.[13]

109. What is medical power of attorney (also known as a "durable power of attorney for health care" or "health-care proxy"), and what are the moral implications of its use?

A medical power of attorney, which may go by different names in different states, is a legal document that is executed if a person cannot make decisions about his medical care. It appoints a trusted person, along with an alternative, to make those decisions if the patient becomes incapacitated. A medical power of attorney does not discuss specific procedures but instead gives someone else the authority to decide on those procedures for the patient. It lasts until a power of attorney is revoked; the principal (patient) is determined to be competent again; or the expiration date of the power of attorney, if one is listed.

Of all the possible types of legal documents that govern end-of-life care, we strongly recommend that readers consider creating and employing a medical power of attorney

---

[13] See especially "A Catholic Guide to End-of-Life Decisions: An Explanation of Church Teaching on Advance Directives, Euthanasia, and Physician Assisted Suicide", available as a PDF download.

in consultation with their legal advisor. For a discussion of how to choose a person to whom to give power of attorney, see Q. 112.

In addition to a medical power of attorney, the authors recommend a supplemental document be created setting forth specific guidelines and instructions for the health-care agent named in the medical power of attorney. Such instructions should specify that the health-care agent must make decisions in accord with the teachings of the Catholic Church. See Appendix V, "Model of 'Catholic Guidelines for Health-Care Agent Appointed by Medical Power of Attorney' ".

110. What is a living will, and what are the relevant moral considerations?

A living will is a type of advance directive. It is a legal document that conveys a person's directions regarding end-of-life treatment and procedures. Its use is so common that there are numerous standardized forms in circulation. Living wills are often written ambiguously and offer morally questionable options in a "check the box" format.

Living wills tend to be imprecise and rigid out of the desire to state with specificity what is to be done and not done in every situation as the end of life draws near. In addition, it is difficult, for example, to determine health-care decisions at age thirty that one intends to apply at the end of life, which may occur decades later.

Another significant problem with a living will is that any ambiguity will be resolved by the treating physician and not the patient's health-care agent. This could mean that the moral formation of the physician rather than a patient's health-care agent will ultimately determine the meaning of a clause or statement capable of more than one interpretation.

While living wills are not inherently immoral, we advise caution in their use (for more on their dangers, see Q. 114). Again, we believe medical power of attorney (see Q. 109) provides superior protection and is a better tool to ensure that a patient's health-care wishes and the Church's teachings are followed. As in all such matters, readers should consult with their attorneys and spiritual advisors.

111. What are physician orders for life-sustaining treatment (POLSTs, also called "medical orders for life-sustaining treatments"), and may they be used?

POLSTs are popular doctor-signed orders (varying in form by state) that are meant to travel with a patient as he moves between health facilities, stating what treatments should be used and withheld when a person is close to the end of life.

The National Catholic Bioethics Center (NCBC) states, "A POLST is a medical order that specifies whether life-sustaining treatment is to be used or withheld for a specific patient in various circumstances. It carries the signatures of the health care provider and sometimes the patient. It differs from a do-not-resuscitate order and a traditional advance directive in that it is actionable from the moment it is signed by the health care provider, even if the patient is still competent and is not terminally ill."[14]

---

[14] Ethicists of the National Catholic Bioethics Center, "Provider Orders for Life-Sustaining Treatments (POLST)", February 2013, rev. 2015, https://static1.squarespace.com/static/5e3ada1a6a2e8d6a131d1dcd/t/5ee135ce6a63940a4b992ae1/1591817679416/NCBCsummFAQ_2013r2015_POLST.pdf.

POLSTs are inherently flawed as a means of morally conveying one's wishes at the end of life, in that they convey a physician's direct orders, which a hospital is bound to follow, regardless of whether a patient's concrete circumstances have changed and regardless of whether the order violates the Church's teachings. Using POLSTs may also result in violations of the USCCB's *Ethical and Religious Directives for Catholic Health Care Services*.[15] For more on the dangers of POLSTs, see the NCBC website.

112. What is a last will and testament or living trust?

A last will and testament is a legal document stating how a person's assets should be distributed at death. It does not address medical care but is an important document to prepare or update for serious illness or death. Alternatively, a living trust is a legal document that establishes a trust that owns one's assets while the person is still alive. Things of value, including real estate, bank accounts, and vehicles, can be placed in a living trust. Upon death, the assets are distributed as outlined in the trust, without the necessity of probate. An attorney should be consulted to discuss the relative benefits of these legal instruments.

113. What is a HIPAA release, and what role does it play in end-of-life decisions?

The Health Insurance Portability and Accountability Act (HIPAA) requires that all medical information be kept confidential by health-care providers. A HIPPA release is a legal document that designates specific individuals (e.g., family members) as persons with whom medical providers

---

[15] National Catholic Bioethics Center, "POLST".

may discuss a patient's medical condition. Signing a HIPAA release form is helpful for seriously ill patients so that their agents and family members can openly discuss health-care information, diagnoses, and prognoses. As with other documents, readers should consult with a legal advisor.

114. What are some of the dangers of relying on an advance directive, such as a living will?

It is impossible for an advance directive such as a living will to anticipate the concrete circumstances of all future medical conditions. What might be ordinary and morally obligatory care for one patient could reasonably be considered extraordinary and thus not mandatory for another patient (e.g., an older adult whose death is imminent).

Since it is impossible to anticipate all possible scenarios, advance directives that opt out of specific medical treatments for unknown future illnesses or conditions can unintentionally provide permission to a medical provider to withhold or withdraw ordinary care when the concrete circumstances are eventually known. For example, a living will stating that the person "does not want artificial nutrition or hydration" could be misused to deny even a simple IV drip of fluids to a patient who may have passed out due to dehydration. Likewise, paramedics who have access to a patient's electronic health records could also misapply a living will to deny medically assisted hydration when a patient is passed out from dehydration due to a superficial urinary tract infection or similar medical problem.

When the advance directive was drafted, the patient may have intended that artificial feeding tubes or fluids not be provided *only* if he is in the end stage of a known terminal illness that makes assimilation of food impossible or medically harmful. But broad pronouncements based on future possibilities and a "check the box" document are incapable of communicating the complexities and intricacies of decisions that may preserve or shorten a patient's life under later circumstances. Even without blanks to fill in and boxes to check, an advance directive in a narrative format setting forth care that is not desired can never adequately anticipate the myriad of factors that go into the art of prudent and moral decision-making and may lead to immoral results.

115. If a doctor's office or a hospital presents me with an advance directive form, should I sign it?

No, unless the advance directive is a medical power of attorney (see QQ. 108–9 above). Many advance directive forms are imprecise and ambiguous. As an alternative, you may consider providing a copy of your medical power of attorney, which should be satisfactory.

The provision of care by doctors and hospitals is not conditioned on a patient providing or signing an advance directive. You cannot be forced to make medical decisions in advance based on speculation, and no patient may be denied care for failure to sign a proposed advance directive.

When one is presented with an advance directive form, we recommend that one consider writing "N/A, see medical power of attorney" in large print across the document.

116. How should I choose a health-care agent?

Whether designated in a medical power of attorney, a durable power of attorney for health care, a health-care proxy, or a similar document by another name, a health-care agent should be someone who is well formed in Catholic teaching. Additionally, he should be someone you trust to make morally sound health-care decisions for you if you cannot speak for yourself. Answering the following few questions may help in the selection of a health-care agent:

Are you confident that the person will be assertive in honoring your wishes and making decisions based on the Church's teachings?

Is the person a knowledgeable and devout Catholic?

Is the person capable of following your guidelines and the teachings of the Church without sentimentality?

Does the person give evidence of the virtues, especially the moral virtues of prudence (wisdom) and fortitude (courage)?

117. What is a "do not resuscitate" (DNR) order, and may I include such instructions in an advance directive or in guidelines for my health-care agent?

A "do not resuscitate" (DNR) order instructs medical personnel not to attempt resuscitation when a patient's heartbeat or breathing ends, which in some circumstances may be morally required ordinary treatment.[16] Therefore, a decision to include DNR instructions in an advance directive or guidelines to one's health-care agent must only be undertaken with prayer and consultation with medical professionals, family, and spiritual advisors.

Any advance directive that includes a DNR must make it explicitly clear that the DNR order may only be applied when morally appropriate, meaning your concrete circumstances must support a finding that resuscitation would

[16] For example, when an otherwise healthy person suffers cardiac arrest. In such circumstance, cardio-pulmonary resuscitation (CPR) would constitute ordinary care since it would likely restore the patient to a reasonably normal life.

be more burdensome than the benefit it would produce
(see QQ. 9–12).

118. May my health-care agent decline or withdraw morally optional treatments or care when my death is imminent, and I am in severe pain?

Yes, provided you could have morally declined or withdrawn the treatments or care if you had not been incapacitated. In other words, a health-care agent may act on
the patient's behalf to decline or withdraw treatments that,
under the circumstances, have been rendered disproportionate or extraordinary (see QQ. 19–20).

The National Catholic Bioethics Center (NCBC) model
health care proxy, available on the NCBC's website, captures the Church's understanding of this concept by including the following language:

> I wish to follow the moral teachings of the Catholic
> Church and to receive all the obligatory care that my faith
> teaches we have a duty to accept. However, I also know
> that death need not be resisted by any and every means
> and that I have the right to refuse medical treatment that is
> excessively burdensome or would only prolong my death
> and delay my being taken to God. I also know that I may
> morally receive medication to relieve pain even if it is
> foreseen that its use may have the unintended result of
> shortening my life.

119. How can I determine the care of my mortal remains upon death?

You may determine the care of your mortal remains
through your last will and testament or the medical power
of attorney. You may also provide written instructions to

your health-care agent. A paragraph may be added to the last will and testament explicitly setting forth the care to be given to one's mortal remains. Here is an example:

> I direct that my body be buried, and not cremated, alongside my beloved spouse, in a decent and Christian manner suitable to my circumstances and condition in life. I further direct that I be buried in accordance with the rites of the Roman Catholic Church.

Additional specifications may be added further explaining the specific care of one's mortal remains. In addition, a paragraph may be inserted into the instructions for one's health-care agent to work closely with one's executor (named in the last will and testament) to ensure the proper care of one's mortal remains.

These determinations and directions may be as straightforward or as detailed as one desires, even to specifying a priest, planning the funeral rites, vigil, and burial, and selecting cemetery property. Many Catholic parishes offer resources to assist in these matters.

120. What moral considerations are there about how my mortal remains should be treated?

You should take whatever measures necessary and possible to ensure that your remains are treated with respect. The Church not only teaches that the dying are to be given attention and care "to help them live their last moments in dignity and peace",[17] but it also requires that "the bodies of the dead must be treated with respect and charity, in

---

[17] *Catechism of the Catholic Church*, no. 2299. This includes that the dying "be helped by the prayer of their relatives, who must see to it that the sick receive at the proper time the sacraments that prepare them to meet the living God".

faith and hope of the Resurrection".[18] Therefore, at every stage, the mortal remains of a Catholic must be treated with the utmost respect. Any acts that may tend, even unintentionally, to insult, violate, or desecrate one's mortal remains must be avoided (see also Q. 122).

121. What plans should be made for my burial?

Catholic burial is a great and holy undertaking. It is a corporal work of mercy and "honors children of God, who are temples of the Holy Spirit".[19]

In August 2016, the Congregation for the Doctrine of the Faith issued its instruction *Ad resurgendum cum Christo* (To rise with Christ),[20] confirming the practice of reverently burying the dead.[21] Burial should be in a sacred place.[22] The reasons that burial of one's mortal remains should occur in a sacred place are that (1) it is "above all the most fitting way to express faith and hope in the resurrection of the body"; (2) it intends to "show the great dignity of the human body"; (3) it corresponds to the piety and respect owed to the bodies of the faithful departed who through Baptism have become temples of the Holy

[18] *Catechism of the Catholic Church*, no. 2300.

[19] *Catechism of the Catholic Church*, no. 2300.

[20] Congregation for the Doctrine of the Faith, Instruction regarding the burial of the deceased and the conservation of the ashes in the case of cremation *Ad resurgendum cum Christo* (October 25, 2016).

[21] Congregation for the Doctrine of the Faith, *Ad resurgendum cum Christo*. The Congregation (then the Holy Office) quoted their 1963 instruction *Piam et constantem*, establishing that "all necessary measures must be taken to preserve the practice of reverently burying the faithful departed", adding, however, that cremation is not "opposed per se to the Christian religion".

[22] See Congregation for the Doctrine of the Faith, *Ad resurgendum cum Christo*, nos. 3, 5. This requirement applies even if cremation is selected. "When, for legitimate motives, cremation of the body has been chosen, the ashes of the faithful must be laid to rest in a sacred place, that is, in a cemetery or, in certain cases, in a church or an area, which has been set aside for this purpose, and so dedicated by the competent ecclesial authority."

Spirit and in which "as instruments and vessels the Spirit has carried out so many good works"; and (4) "the burial of the faithful departed in cemeteries or other sacred places encourages family members and the whole Christian community to pray for and remember the dead, while at the same time fostering the veneration of martyrs and saints."[23] For these reasons, the Church has historically declined to condone treatment of mortal remains that include attitudes, actions, or rites involving false ideas about death.[24]

The Church's funeral rites,[25] which give great comfort to the faithful, have developed over the centuries to evoke reverently the soul's passage from this life to the heavenly Jerusalem. These rites should be consulted in total and should guide the plans for one's mortal remains. The following is a condensed summary to highlight the reverential treatment of mortal remains:

> Prayers after death: These are prayers offered at the time of death or shortly after that. A priest or deacon typically leads them, and they customarily take place bedside, whether in a hospital, a nursing facility, or the private home of the deceased.
>
> Vigil (wake): This usually takes place the evening before the Funeral Liturgy, either in the funeral home or the church. It is the principal rite celebrated by the faithful

---

[23] Congregation for the Doctrine of the Faith, *Ad resurgendum cum Christo*, no. 3. The quotation "as instruments and vessels the Spirit has carried out so many good works" is from St. Augustine, *De cura pro mortuis gerenda*.

[24] Congregation for the Doctrine of the Faith, *Ad resurgendum cum Christo*, no. 3, including, but not limited to, "considering death as the definitive annihilation of the person, or the moment of fusion with Mother Nature or the universe, or as a stage in the cycle of regeneration, or as the definitive liberation from the 'prison' of the body".

[25] See the Roman Ritual, *Order of Christian Funerals*; see also Adrian Fortescue and J. O'Connell, *The Ceremonies of the Roman Rite Described*, 6th edition (London: Burns Oates and Washbourne, 1937), 444–64.

following death and before the Funeral Mass.[26] The traditional and pious devotional of praying the Rosary differs from this rite. The Vigil is the official prayer of the Church, and it may take the form of a Liturgy of the Word or a form of the Office of the Dead from the Liturgy of the Hours.

Funeral Mass: All Catholics are entitled to a Funeral Mass, which should generally be celebrated in the deceased's parish church.[27]

Rite of Committal (burial): The body is interred at a cemetery in sacred ground or a mausoleum.

122. As a Catholic, may I choose to be cremated?

Yes. However, your ashes must still be preserved in a sacred place, preferably by burial.[28] The Church prefers the practice of burial of the body because it shows greater esteem for the deceased. Nonetheless, it permits cremation for legitimate sanitary, economic, and social reasons, as long as it does not violate the explicitly stated or the reasonably inferable wishes of the deceased faithful[29] and is not chosen for reasons contrary to Christian doctrine.[30] Also, cremation should normally occur after the Catholic

[26] See *Order of Christian Funerals*, 54.

[27] There is a Funeral Liturgy Outside Mass if, for some reason, it is impossible to have a Funeral Mass.

[28] Congregation for the Doctrine of the Faith, *Ad resurgendum cum Christo*, no. 5: "The ashes of the faithful must be laid to rest in a sacred place, that is, in a cemetery or, in certain cases, in a church or an area, which has been set aside for this purpose, and so dedicated by the competent ecclesial authority."

[29] Congregation for the Doctrine of the Faith, *Ad resurgendum cum Christo*, no. 5.

[30] Congregation for the Doctrine of the Faith, *Ad resurgendum cum Christo*, no. 5. Motives the CDF considers legitimate include "circumstances when cremation is chosen because of sanitary, economic or social considerations".

funeral rites and with special care "to avoid every form of scandal or the appearance of religious indifferentism".[31]

Cremation of the body does not affect the soul or prevent its rise to new life at the resurrection. In practice, however, it can lead to irreverence and even the desecration of the mortal remains of human beings. Thus, the Church prohibits the preservation of the departed's ashes in a private residence, and it further prohibits the practice of dividing the departed's ashes among various family members.[32]

In particular, to avoid "every appearance of pantheism, naturalism or nihilism", the Church prohibits the scattering of the ashes of the faithful departed "in the air, on land, at sea or in some other way", or having the departed's ashes preserved "in mementos, pieces of jewellery or other objects".[33] Under certain circumstances, a deceased Catholic who requested cremation and the scattering of their ashes must be denied a Christian funeral.[34]

123. May a Catholic donate his body to scientific research or donate his organs at the time of death?

Yes. The Church recognizes that scientific research on the body and donation of organs can contribute to healing

[31] Congregation for the Doctrine of the Faith, *Ad resurgendum cum Christo*, no. 5. "Indifferentism" in this context may be understood as any manner, action, or practice that could give the impression that the Catholic faith is untrue or that one religion and its practices is as good as another.

[32] Congregation for the Doctrine of the Faith, *Ad resurgendum cum Christo*, no. 6. Only in "grave and exceptional cases dependent on cultural conditions of a localized nature" may special permission for the conservation of the ashes of the departed in a domestic residence be granted.

[33] Congregation for the Doctrine of the Faith, *Ad resurgendum cum Christo*, no. 7.

[34] Congregation for the Doctrine of the Faith, *Ad resurgendum cum Christo*, no. 8. "When the deceased notoriously has requested cremation and the scattering of their ashes for reasons contrary to the Christian faith."

the sick and advancing public health. It may even be meritorious.[35] The donation of the deceased's body for scientific research is also allowed.[36] It is, however, an illusion to presume scientific research and the harvesting and use of human organs are morally neutral.[37] Due to the absence of moral neutrality and considering modern threats to life at every stage, caution is in order in planning for the donation of one's organs (see Q. 42).

First, the Church makes clear that explicit consent of the donor (or his proxy) is required. Also, it is immoral to mutilate a person or prematurely bring about his death even to help another person live longer.[38] This is why properly donated organs should not "be removed until it has been medically determined that the patient has died"[39] by a physician or competent medical authority, by responsible and commonly accepted scientific criteria.

Second, the removal of organs should not cause the patient's death. It is fundamental Catholic moral teaching that one may never do evil (e.g., kill a patient, even if death is imminent) to do good (procure an organ for transplant into a needy patient). A good intention cannot nullify the inherent evil of an action. Thus, the donor patient must be irreversibly dead before any attempt may be made to secure an organ or tissue. In other words, there must be a corpse and not a living, albeit an ill and dying, human being as the source of the organ or tissue.

Third, to prevent any conflict of interest, "the physician who determines death should not be a member of the

[35] See Catechism of the Catholic Church, nos. 2292, 2296, 2301.

[36] Catechism of the Catholic Church, no. 2301: "Autopsies can be morally permitted for legal inquests or scientific research." After the research is complete, respect for the body and burial in a sacred space would apply to the remains.

[37] See Catechism of the Catholic Church, no. 2294.

[38] See Catechism of the Catholic Church, no. 2296.

[39] United States Conference of Catholic Bishops, Ethical and Religious Directives for Catholic Health Care Services, no. 64.

transplant team".[40] This limitation is designed to ensure that a disinterested medical professional makes a good-faith determination of death. It is also an additional safeguard to prevent a loved one from being killed.

Fourth, the donated organs must be used for "ethically legitimate purposes". Saving the life of another person in need (e.g., through a kidney or liver transplant) or allowing them to regain a sense (e.g., through cornea transplant) are moral purposes. On the other hand, the use of transplanted organs or tissues for the creation of an animal-human chimeric embryo would be an immoral purpose.

Finally, using tissue or organs from an infant after death is permitted only "with the informed consent of the parents or guardian".[41]

With respect to a donation after death of bodily remains for medical research or teaching (e.g., a medical school anatomy class), we strongly encourage a donor or donor's family to enter into a written agreement with the medical research facility or medical school that expressly requires that after the research or teaching is completed, the donated body be returned to the donor's family for interment in sacred ground or a church-dedicated mausoleum. Alternatively, if the donor's family prefers, the agreement should state that the donor's body be cremated, and the cremated remains are to be returned to the donor's family for burial or proper disposition in sacred ground or a church-dedicated mausoleum.

[40] United States Conference of Catholic Bishops, *Ethical and Religious Directives for Catholic Health Care Services*, no. 64.

[41] United States Conference of Catholic Bishops, *Ethical and Religious Directives for Catholic Health Care Services*, no. 65.

ACKNOWLEDGMENTS

We thank our editors, Vivian Dudro and Abigail Tardiff, for their close attention to the progress of the book and whose comments and suggested edits improved the final product. We also thank those who conducted presubmission reviews of the initial draft of the book and offered encouraging comments and suggestions. Particular mention is due to Professor John Bauer, Ph.D., for his meticulous presubmission review of the initial draft of the manuscript. His background in moral philosophy and his insightful questions and comments helped refine and simplify some complex ideas. He undertook this task on short notice and with a new semester of teaching approaching, and we are grateful.

APPENDIX I

The Principle of Double Effect and Its Application in End-of-Life Decisions

What is meant by the "principle of double effect"?

Although he did not use the specific term, Saint Thomas Aquinas is credited with introducing the principle of double effect.[1] Through the centuries, the Catholic Church has used the principle of double effect to help discern the rightness or wrongness of actions that will have both good and evil results.[2] The principle, supported in the Bible and natural law, permits actions with a double effect, good and bad, under certain conditions.

Under what specific conditions may the principle of double effect be used to make decisions between acts with both good and bad results?

An example of the principle of double effect in the context of end-of-life issues is the administration of painkillers or sedatives to relieve pain and suffering, with the foreseeable but unintended effect that the patient's life may be shortened.

When an action or decision has two effects, one good and one evil, it may be done only if it meets the following four conditions:

---

[1] See Thomas Aquinas, *Summa Theologiae*, II-II, q. 64, a. 7.
[2] See, e.g., *Catechism of the Catholic Church*, no. 2263.

The act must be good in itself or at least morally indiffer-
ent. It thus must not be intrinsically evil (that is, an act that
can never be morally justified, regardless of the intention
of the person who performs it).

The good effect must not come about by means of the evil
effect. Any evil effect that occurs must only be a consequence of the good effect and inseparable from it.

The evil effect must not be intended (no bad will may
exist).

There must be a proportionately grave reason for permitting the evil effect (or, at least, the good and evil effects
should be nearly equal).[3]

If an action has two effects, one good and one bad, all
four of the above conditions must be met; otherwise, the
act is morally wrong.

How does the principle of double effect apply in the context of end-of-life decisions?

Some moral questions that arise in treating serious illness
or incurable disease call for a consideration of the principle
of double effect.

In making treatment decisions, neither the physician,
patient, nor family members may decide to take an intrinsically evil action. No amount of good intention, compassion, or mercy can overcome an inherently evil act, such
as euthanasia, suicide, or assisted suicide.

In all decisions, the physician's, the patient's, and the family members' intention must be morally good. Sometimes,
particularly in the context of the relief of suffering through

---

[3] John Hardon, *Modern Catholic Dictionary* (Garden City, NY: Doubleday,
1980), s.v. "Double effect", 171.

painkillers and sedatives, the intended good effect (relief from pain) also has a potential bad effect that is foreseen but unintended. In such situations, the principle of double effect will determine whether an action may be done or not.

An example of the above is a hospitalized patient with advanced and incurable pancreatic cancer that has spread to his bones, causing excruciating pain. Physicians confirm that the patient is terminally ill, but they cannot predict how long he may live. Doctors have for some time prescribed standard pain medications that now appear to have no effect because of a built-up tolerance on the part of the patient. The physicians have advised the patient and his family that the only way to alleviate his pain is to administer higher and higher doses of morphine. A reasonably foreseeable effect of administering higher doses of morphine is the likelihood that the patient's death may be hastened. The patient has pleaded for relief from the pain in prior lucid moments. The pain has become constant, and the family members are faced with the question of whether to allow the increased doses of palliative medicine, even though it may hasten death.

Analysis: Regarding condition (a) (that the act itself must not be evil), the administration of morphine is a good (or at least neutral) act because it relieves the patient's excruciating pain and is not intrinsically evil.

Regarding condition (b) (the evil effect must not be a means to the good effect), the good effect of relieving pain is not the result of the hastening of death but the nature of the medication itself. Moreover, the evil effect of a hastened death is only a consequence of the good effect and is inseparable from it.

Regarding condition (c) (the evil effect must not be intended), the hastening of death is not intended. What is intended is the relief of intolerable pain.

Finally, regarding condition (d) (there must be a proportionate reason for allowing the evil effect), the relief of excruciating pain is a proportionately grave reason for permitting the foreseeable but unintended evil of a hastened death. In this case, the requirement of a proportionate reason is met insofar as the patient's death is inevitable and impending, and the last remaining option to relieve the patient's intolerable pain is the administration of higher doses of morphine.

APPENDIX II

The Formation of Conscience

The operation of one's conscience may be simply described as an act of the mind that tells one what is right or wrong in a particular situation. It does this by approving or disapproving a specific action, either by peace of mind or remorse.

However, making sound decisions about right and wrong in particular situations requires a well-formed conscience. Every person is responsible for selecting the proper means of forming his conscience in truth.[1] Since only a well-formed conscience ought to be followed, it is essential to know how this formation will take place.

Conscience is an act of judgment (see Q. 51), so the question becomes, How does a person develop a well-formed "act of judgment"? A very simplified answer is that one achieves this capacity in two ways: (1) by internally developing virtue as a habit and (2) by externally increasing God's influence on one's moral acts and decisions and decreasing the Devil's influence on one's moral acts and decisions.[2]

The Catholic Church does not require any specific approach to the formation of conscience. Instead, the process comes from a living tradition that transmits the teachings and disciplines necessary to develop a well-formed

[1] See *Catechism of the Catholic Church*, no. 1783.
[2] See Vernon J. Bourke, *Ethics: A Textbook in Moral Philosophy* (New York: Macmillan, 1966), especially chapter 7 (discussion on the virtues and moral character).

conscience. The Church provides this tradition, which has developed over its two-thousand-year history. The specific means that may be employed come from the Church's teachings and disciplines, like those used in spiritual formation and growth.

Formation Begins with the Elementary Principles of Conscience

As J. Budziszewski well illustrates, the idea that we must remain neutral on the question of whether an act is morally good or evil out of "tolerance" is an illusion at best.[3] He points out that we call certain things like murder and rape evil not merely because we choose to make them so but because we *already know* they are wrong.[4] The evil of these things is presupposed and comes from an infused and deep-seated moral sense that communicates to our conscience that certain evils are among the things that cannot *not* be known.

This moral sense, which is also called "natural law",[5] is infused into our soul by God at conception.[6] Saint Paul describes it as written on the heart.[7] But it is just a beginning. This interior sense of right and wrong provides the elementary principles of the moral law that can be known by reason, but these principles must be enlarged, built upon, and explained. This process, along with growth in

---

[3] J. Budziszewski, *The Revenge of Conscience: Politics and the Fall of Man* (Dallas, TX: Spence Publishing, 199), 39–54.

[4] Budziszewski, *Revenge of Conscience*, 9.

[5] Because it has the qualities of law, and it is built into the design of human nature.

[6] See *Catechism of the Catholic Church*, no. 1776.

[7] Rom 2:15: "What the law requires is written on their hearts."

knowledge of the teaching of revelation, helps the conscience formulate its judgments according to reason and conform to the teachings of the Christian faith. In other words, it develops a well-formed conscience.

Fortunately, we are not meant to work this process out by ourselves. The formation of the conscience begins early and is a lifelong process. It starts in childhood with a recognition of an interior moral sense of right and wrong. The early years of building upon and enlarging the elementary principles of conscience come from parental instruction. The development of conscience also comes from the living tradition of the Church that transmits both the teachings and disciplines necessary to develop a well-formed conscience.

The remainder of this appendix suggests specific internal and external means of building upon the elementary principles of conscience to develop a mature, well-formed conscience.

Means for Developing a Well-Formed Conscience

A well-formed conscience requires an educational process and appropriate means. These means may be internal or external.

The first internal means is a sincere desire to achieve a well-formed conscience.

In the supernatural order, our good desires are influenced by God's grace. Thus, the desire to have a well-formed conscience involves a person making an act of the will, under the influence of grace, to seek the spiritual progress of a conscience formed by truth. This desire comes from the combined action of God's grace and human will.

Desire for a well-formed conscience can be quickened by giving attention to several sources. The Holy Scriptures, especially the Gospels and the Epistles, inspire a desire for spiritual growth and a conscience responsive to the moral law. The Church's liturgy, which in the course of the liturgical year sets forth our Lord's life, makes us express the longing for union with Christ and his kingdom. Thus, the liturgy can quicken our desire for moral formation and spiritual growth. Inspiration can also be gained from reading the lives of the saints and witnessing their desire for moral perfection. Finally, faithful prayer to God for a purer and greater desire for spiritual growth and a conscience sensitive to moral truth will increase our desire.

The second internal means of developing a well-formed conscience is docility to the moral law and the teachings of the Church.

The word "docility" comes from the Latin word *docilitas*, which means the capacity of being taught or teachableness. It is more than native intellectual ability; it is a certain humility and desire to receive instruction. Just as a child needs to be docile to the teaching of his parents, a Catholic needs to be docile to the moral law and desire to be taught its truth by the Magisterium of the Church. The Church possesses the fullness of truth, and any confusion about that fact or resistance to it will make the moral formation of conscience difficult.

There is nothing more harmful to the moral formation of conscience than seeking our own will rather than God's will. Thus, moral formation requires an interior openness to guidance outside ourselves—a longing for received truth. This is true for spiritual formation generally but even more so for moral formation, where the growth process necessarily involves confrontations between conscience and moral law. When those confrontations occur, we must be teachable and receptive to the truth when it is presented to us.

Of the external means of developing a well-formed conscience, the first is spiritual direction.

Spiritual direction is "the guidance voluntarily sought by a person intent on progress in the spiritual life".[8] Spiritual direction is not an absolute necessity for developing a well-formed conscience, but it is one of the ordinary means of spiritual progress.[9]

We cannot be impartial judges in our own cases, and it is easy to deceive oneself regarding one's spiritual condition. We also tend toward a complacency that is difficult to see in ourselves even with the keenest insight. Spiritual direction from a trusted and well-formed spiritual advisor can provide insights, instruction, and advice on ways to improve the formation of one's conscience.

In addition to orthodoxy with regard to Catholic doctrine, qualities to look for in a spiritual director include *charity*, *kindness* (but not weakness; a spiritual director must be firm and frank), *sound judgment* (that is, the gift of counsel), and *knowledge* (of moral theology).[10]

The second external means of developing a well-formed conscience is adopting a rule of life.

This is an expression we do not often hear these days, but it is difficult to improve on the term once we understand it. The word "rule" comes from the Latin word *regula* and

[8] John Hardon, *Modern Catholic Dictionary* (Garden City, NY: Doubleday, 1980), s.v. "Direction, spiritual", 159.

[9] Adolphe Tanquerey, *The Spiritual Life: A Treatise on Ascetical and Mystical Theology* (New York: Desclee, 1930), 257.

[10] Tanquerey, *Spiritual Life*, 264–65.

suggests a way of ordering our lives so that we can stay on the path toward our ultimate end. A rule of life is common for those in religious life. The methods of living the evangelical counsels are called "rules", like the Rule of Saint Augustine or the Rule of Saint Benedict.

As used here, a "rule of life" refers to a voluntary customary standard that regulates a person's conduct for more effective spiritual growth and moral living. It is the formal structure for the transmission of the Church's tradition—its teachings and disciplines. It is a set of guidelines that support or enable us to do the things we need to do to reach spiritual maturity and a well-formed conscience.

The formation of a good conscience does not happen by itself. There must be a framework in place to transmit the tradition of the Church in its teachings and disciplines. This is where a rule of life comes in. A rule of life helps us by providing a plan for spiritual growth and moral formation. It also enables us to make good use of our time and to develop supernatural motives for all our actions.

A rule of life should be developed with the help of a spiritual director if possible. It should be *firm* enough to direct the will, but *flexible* enough to adapt to real-life circumstances. It should reflect *prudence* and not lay down spiritual exercises too numerous or too advanced for the individual. Finally, it should reflect a *hierarchy* in spiritual duties. God must hold first place, then the welfare of our soul and our neighbor, always displaying a balance between prayer and action.

The elements of a rule of life will differ among individuals—there is no such thing as one rule of life that fits all. At a minimum, a rule life that transmits the tradition of the Church's teachings and disciplines should include an ordered approach to prayer, regular religious duties, spiritual reading and study, and a plan for growth in the virtues.

The Catholic Church has a rich store of devotional practices and prayers, many of which may be incorporated into a rule of life. Regular practices, daily prayer, Mass, confession, and spiritual reading are critical elements of a rule that will help form conscience.

Common Causes of Poor Formation of Conscience

It is sobering to realize that it is possible to have a false conscience (that is, one not in conformity with the moral law) or to set one's conscience aside. The conscience can also be darkened by widespread societal conditioning so that it is hard to discern good from evil.[11]

The judgment of conscience, if set aside, can become defiled. If it is persistently set aside, it becomes hardened or seared (see Q. 53). In such a situation, a person can justify the most unthinkable and immoral decisions, even murdering while believing he is offering a service to God (see Jn 16:2).

A detailed analysis of the causes for such a corruption of conscience is beyond the scope of this appendix and book. Still, it is helpful to be alert to some of the apparent reasons for poor or distorted formation of conscience mentioned in the *Catechism of the Catholic Church*:[12]

Ignorance of Christ and his Gospel

The bad example given by others (this can also include poor instruction by laypeople and clerics)

Enslavement to one's passions

---

[11] John Paul II, encyclical letter *Evangelium vitae* (The Gospel of Life) (March 25, 1995), no. 4.

[12] See *Catechism of the Catholic Church*, no. 1762.

Assertion of a mistaken notion of the autonomy of conscience

Rejection of the Church's authority and her teaching

Lack of conversion and charity (Two dangerous vices contrary to charity are discord, the knowing and intentional dissent from the Divine Good and the good of one's neighbor, and schism, the lack of submission to the authority of the Church.)

If personal struggles exist with a distorted or troublesome conscience, it may be helpful to engage in an examination of conscience under the guidance of spiritual direction, using the list above as a starting point.

Resources for Spiritual Reading to Help in the Formation of Conscience

Veritatis splendor by John Paul II, encyclical letter, August 6, 1993: responds to the crisis in Christian moral theology in the aftermath of the Second Vatican Council.

Evangelium vitae by John Paul II, encyclical letter, March 25, 1995: defends human life by denouncing the dangers of a "culture of death" and condemning abortion, euthanasia, and suicide.

Samaritanus bonus by the Congregation for the Doctrine of the Faith, July 14, 2020: addresses the care of persons in the critical and terminal phases of life.

Declaration on Euthanasia by the Congregation for the Doctrine of the Faith, May 5, 1980: addresses questions posed by advances in medical technology.

Donum vitae by the Congregation for the Doctrine of the Faith, February 22, 1987: considers questions raised by biotechnology.

A Map of Life: A Simple Study of the Catholic Faith by Frank Sheed: a short explanation of the Catholic faith by one of the most precise writers of the twentieth century.

The 12 Steps to Holiness and Salvation: From the Works of St. Alphonsus Liguori: a short but powerful volume made up of choice selections on the virtues from the ascetical writings of Saint Alphonsus Liguori.

The Way of Perfection by Saint Teresa of Avila: written by a saint and doctor of the Church whose work on prayer is significantly referenced in Part Four, "Christian Prayer", of the *Catechism of the Catholic Church.*

Spiritual Combat: How to Win Your Spiritual Battles and Attain Inner Peace by Lorenzo Scupoli: a great spiritual classic that has influenced Catholic spirituality for four hundred years. Saint Francis de Sales carried a copy of this book in his pocket for eighteen years.

Spiritual Combat Revisited by Jonathan Robinson: a very well-written reworking of Scupoli's masterpiece for modern Catholics that covers the main points of the original and more.

Cultivating Virtue: Self-Mastery with the Saints by an anonymous author: get the 2019 reprint of the first edition published in 1891. This book was originally entitled *A Year with the Saints* and is a devotional manual that takes up a different virtue each month to encourage the practice of self-examination regarding the virtues. Very helpful to the moral formation of the conscience.

Back to Virtue: Traditional Moral Wisdom for Modern Moral Confusion by Peter Kreeft: a very insightful work on the virtues in the modern context that is scripturally and theologically sound. Kreeft applies traditional moral theology to contemporary moral questions, which is particularly helpful in the process of moral decision-making.

Learning the Virtues: That Lead You to God by Romano Guardini: written by a priest regarded highly by Pope Benedict XVI. The author highlights the necessity of doing more than simply keeping the Ten Commandments; one must also cultivate virtue. This book serves as a guide on how to do that.

My Daily Bread by Father Anthony J. Paone: a series of short daily reflections on the spiritual and moral life. This pocket-size book will help increase and strengthen your love for Christ and his teachings.

The Moral Dignity of Man by Peter Bristow: a broader and more detailed treatment of Catholic moral doctrine than that presented in this book, focusing on family and medical ethics.

Our Moral Life in Christ: A Basic Course on Moral Theology by Aurelio Fernández and James Socias: an excellent and detailed introductory course in moral theology, formation, and conscience.

Spiritual Theology by Father Jordan Aumann, O.P.: an excellent work on spiritual theology that contains detailed explanations of the virtues and their relation to moral formation. The author's discussion of the temperaments and their effect on formation is constructive.

APPENDIX III

Annotated Resources for Further Study

Any list of written resources for spiritual study will necessarily be incomplete, born of the experiences of its compilers and subject to their prejudices. This includes the current appendix. The compilers have, however, focused on resources that bear directly on spiritual and moral formation, with a particular emphasis on resources that are practical and accessible to laypeople. These resources are familiar and have proven practically beneficial to the compilers. In short, they are recommended from experience.

Many excellent resources are available that are not included on this list. We direct readers to two more general and extensive lists that may be of interest in the future: (1) *A Catholic Lifetime Reading Plan* by Father John Hardon, S.J., and (2) The Catholic Information Center Lifetime Reading Plan.

Recommended Resources That Deal Directly with Preparation for Serious Illness and Dying

The Art of Dying: A New Annotated Translation by Anonymous, trans. Brother Columba Thomas, O.P., MD. This is an excellent recent translation by the National Catholic Bioethics Center of the *Ars moriendi*, a work originally published in the late Middle Ages. The introduction by the translator is very helpful in understanding the *Ars moriendi* and its application to preparation for a good death, mainly because the experience of dying can seriously test one's faith and must be anticipated. In addition to the text explaining the most common temptations of the Devil at the hour of a person's death (and the way to respond to them), there are prayers to be prayed at the bedside of the dying, as well as several helpful appendices. The compilers recommend this book as the go-to handbook for bedside prayers for the dying Catholic, along with the prayers in *My Prayer Book* by Father F. X. Lasance, beginning with the Prayer for a Happy Death by Cardinal Newman.

The Art of Dying Well: How to Be a Saint Now and Forever by Saint Robert Bellarmine, originally published in Latin in Rome in 1620, with the first English translation appearing in 1622. This edition (Sophia Institute Press) is a modern republication and contains Book 1 of Bellarmine's original work, except Chapter 17, which is taken from Book 2. It is perhaps the best and most practical guide for Catholics who want to prepare to die well by living well now. The compilers recommend this book as the helpful go-to guide for spiritual preparation before serious illness and death.

Preparation for Death: Considerations on Eternal Truths by Saint Alphonsus Liguori. This is a classic and timeless manual by a great saint on living in preparation for eternity. It is easy to read and excellent in every respect. The compilers generally recommend it as a short but effective treatment of a subject heard little about these days—the reality of hell and how to avoid it.

The Lost Art of Dying: Reviving Forgotten Wisdom by L. S. Dugdale, MD. This is not a religious book that offers guidance for spiritual or moral formation. Still, it uses the *Ars moriendi* to develop an approach based on traditional wisdom to illness and dying. The book offers many practical insights that can help patients overcome medicalized and institutional dying tendencies.

Recommended Resources for Firming Up One's Knowledge of the Catholic Faith

The Penny Catechism by Anonymous. A clear and simple approach to learning the basics of the Catholic faith. With over three hundred concise questions and answers, this is a profoundly helpful little work. While there are numerous catechisms[1] that are helpful, we recommend this work for daily reference in a lay Catholic's sound rule of life (see Appendix II). The present book's question-and-answer format is loosely based on the approach of *The Penny Catechism*.

Baltimore Catechism No. 3 by Rev. Francis J. Connell, C.SS.R. *The Baltimore Catechism* was prepared by decree of the Third Council of Baltimore. *Baltimore Catechism No. 3* uses a question-and-answer format, study helps, and Biblical references to illustrate the Scriptural foundation of the

---

[1] There are two *universal* catechisms in the Catholic Church: *The Roman Catechism* (also known as the *Catechism of the Council of Trent*) and the *Catechism of the Catholic Church*. A "universal catechism" is a major catechism intended to be a resource or point of reference for developing national or local catechisms and catechetical materials worldwide. Such a catechism can be termed "universal" because its primary audience is the universal Church (see "Frequently Asked Questions about the Catechism of the Catholic Church", United States Conference of Catholic Bishops, https://www.usccb.org/committees/subcommittee-catechism/faq-about-catechism). There are, however, other catechisms helpful in specific ways. For average Catholic laypeople, we recommend *The Penny Catechism* for its brevity and accessibility and *The Baltimore Catechism No. 3* for its study helps and references to Holy Scripture. For those with more time and interest, we recommend either universal catechism, both of which are longer and helpful in finding in-depth explanations.

Catholic faith. In conjunction with *The Penny Catechism*, this outstanding catechism will provide laypeople with a basic and comprehensive knowledge of Catholic teachings.

Theology and Sanity by Frank Sheed. This is one of the best and clearest modern treatments of Catholic theology available in print. It is written by a lay Catholic apologist (defender of the faith) gifted in simplifying and clarifying theological teachings. Sheed explains several important matters explored in *Now and at the Hour of Our Death*. He includes a very good treatment of the reality and meaning of suffering, perceptively stating, "The chief problem of suffering is how not to waste it."[2]

The Belief of Catholics by Father Ronald Knox. This timeless classic was initially published in 1927, and Ignatius Press republished it in 2000. It contains references to English Catholicism throughout but is recommended as one of the best modern works on what it means to think and believe as a Catholic. Intended for the intelligent lay Catholic, it is written with the seamless development of apologetics for which Father Knox was famous. He discusses "the truths Catholics hold", "the rules Catholics acknowledge", and "the strength Catholics receive", among many other exceptional chapters.

Recommended Resources for a Deeper Spiritual Formation

Ignatius Bible (RSV), 2nd Edition. A growing familiarity with and understanding of the Holy Scripture is necessary

---

[2] Frank J. Sheed, *Theology and Sanity* (London: Bloomsbury Academic, 1978), 304.

for any sound spiritual formation. This version of the Bible is a clear and accurate translation, without the use of "inclusive language". It is excellent for daily use in reading portions of the Old Testament and New Testament.

New Testament, Confraternity Edition, Pocket Size. A reliable reprint of the Confraternity edition published in 1941. Readings are short and presented for every day of the year. Although the book is pocket-sized, the type is large enough to read with ease. The authors recommend this edition for daily use in meditation.

The Soul of the Apostolate by Jean-Baptiste Chautard, O.C.S.O. While of particular interest to those who do apostolic work (the work of bringing people to the knowledge and love of Christ), this is the best book available for demonstrating that the foundation of Christian life and of all apostolic work must be the interior life. It makes it clear that Christian formation only comes about through prayer, meditation, and the cultivation of the interior life. It is a very practical work that is instrumental in developing a rule of life.

Introduction to the Devout Life by Saint Francis de Sales, C.O., O.F.M. This is a classic guidebook to deeper life in God by one of the most influential figures on the founders of the seventeenth century French Catholic school of spirituality.

The Fulfillment of All Desire: A Guidebook for the Journey to God Based on the Wisdom of the Saints by Ralph Martin. A modern work that draws upon the teaching of seven Doctors of the Church to feed the deep desire to journey toward God. It also introduces the reader to the rich patrimony of the Church for spiritual direction. An excellent book for seriously spiritually hungry beginners.

Self-Abandonment to Divine Providence by Father Jean-Pierre de Caussade. This book has life-changing potential to help one see how every moment and event can be sanctifying. This work will help one look at suffering from an entirely different perspective. "There is no moment at which God does not present Himself under the guise of some suffering, of some consolation or some duty. All that occurs within us, around us and by our means covers and hides His divine action."[3]

Trustful Surrender to Divine Providence by Father. Jean Baptiste Saint Jure, S.J., and Saint Claude de la Colombière, S.J. This short but powerful spiritual work contains two extracts from larger works by the two authors. It addresses trust in God and surrender to his providence in times of loss, sickness, infirmity, and death.

[3] Fr. Jean-Pierre de Caussade, *Self-Abandonment to Divine Providence and Letters of Father de Caussade on the Practice of Self-Abandonment*, trans. Algar Thorold, ed. Fr. John Joyce, S.J. (Charlotte, NC: TAN Books, 1959), p. 18.

APPENDIX IV

Glossary

Advance directive. A legal document prepared before a medical crisis to convey one's directions about end-of-life care (see QQ. 113–15).

Aggressive medical treatments. Medical procedures on patients whose death is imminent and inevitable that would be disproportionate to any expected results or would impose an excessive burden on the patient and his family (see Q. 22).

Ambiguity. As used in this book, this term refers to a situation or statement whose meaning is capable of more than one interpretation. Ambiguous terms or statements are imprecise and open to misunderstanding.

Ars moriendi. The *ars moriendi* is the "art of dying", that is, the wisdom of living well and dying well—of pursuing ultimate happiness—that comes from centuries of Catholic teaching and culture. Specifically, the phrase comes from one of the most popular books of the late Middle Ages, written by an anonymous Dominican friar (see QQ. 3, 102–3).

Autonomy. As commonly used in modern society, autonomy is the idea that each person decides right and wrong for himself, without interference from external forces (see Q. 68). This common use is distinguished from legitimate autonomy, which is the freedom to decide a course of action in a way that is guided by reason and truth (see Q. 69).

Basic or ordinary care. The nonmedical care required for every human being to sustain life and provide comfort in illness (see Q. 15).

Body. The body is the physical, material substance of a human or animal. The human body is thus the physical substance—the mortal aspect of man (see Q. 35).

Brain death. The complete and irreversible loss of all upper and lower brain stem functions. It is also called the determination of death by neurological criteria (see Q. 39).

Burden. As used in this book, the term "burden" is not a judgment or assessment of the value of a person. It is a practical term used in the decision-making process to help assess whether a proposed medical treatment is objectively beneficial or onerous (overly troublesome) to the patient. If consideration of the concrete circumstances of the patient indicates that a proposed treatment will be more burdensome to the patient or his family than beneficial to him, the specific medical treatment is not morally required (see QQ. 9–10).

Burial. The action of interring one's mortal remains in a grave or tomb (see Q. 121).

Cardiopulmonary criteria. The use of the conditions of irreversible cessation of circulatory and respiratory functions to determine when death occurs (see Q. 38).

Comatose. Being in a state of deep unconsciousness for a prolonged or indefinite period, especially due to severe injury or illness.

Concrete circumstances. The concrete circumstances of an individual patient are the factors used to determine whether a particular medical treatment offers a reasonable hope of benefit and does not entail an excessive burden or expense. The concrete circumstances of a patient describe his condition or situation and include, among other factors, his age, whether his death is considered imminent and unpreventable, whether he is in severe or intolerable pain, whether the treatment will realistically offer a lasting improvement in his condition or prognosis, the risks and side effects of the treatment, his financial condition, and the financial impact on the patient and the family (see Q. 11).

Concupiscence. Concupiscence is a result of our fallen nature that makes us prone to evil rather than to good. It is an inclination to yield to wrong rather than to resist it. As used in this book, "concupiscence" refers to the strong internal desire in every person to subordinate the dictates of reason to one's desires (whether those desires are an inordinate love of the world's goods or the inordinate love of sensual pleasures). Concupiscence comes from original sin, remains in a person while in this life, and tends to attract a person toward whatever he believes is pleasant and away from whatever he concludes is unpleasant or painful.

Conscience. An act of reason and judgment by which a person uses his mind to apply his knowledge of right and wrong to a specific course of action (see Q. 51).

Cost (economic). In the context of this book, "cost" refers to economic impact—specifically, the economic impact of medical treatments on a patient and his family. It is only one criterion to consider in making moral end-of-life decisions (see Q. 29).

Cremation. The process of reducing the physical body to ashes and bone fragments through intense heat. These cremated remains are then crushed to break up larger bone fragments to a granular texture (see Q. 122).

Death. With regard to humans, death is the irreversible cessation of the bodily functions that occurs when the soul departs the body (see Q. 34).

Dignity. As used in this book, "dignity" refers to the intrinsic worth of a human being that results from his being created in the image and likeness of God. In modern society, the word often occurs in the phrase "death with dignity" to signify physician-assisted suicide and euthanasia (see QQ. 71, 104).

Disproportionate and extraordinary. As used in this book, these terms refer to medical treatments or interventions that do not offer a reasonable hope of benefit to a patient (see Q. 19).

DNR (do not resuscitate). An order contained in an advance directive (or in guidelines to a health-care agent) that instructs medical personnel not to attempt resuscitation when the patient's heartbeat or breathing ends (see Q. 117).

Euthanasia. An act or a failure to act that is intended to cause death so that suffering may be eliminated (see Q. 45).

Extraordinary. See Disproportionate and extraordinary.

Feeding tube. A medical device used to provide nutrition or hydration to a patient who cannot take nutrition and hydration by mouth, cannot swallow safely, or needs nutritional supplementation (see Q. 18).

Futile care. There is no current consensus among medical professionals as to the meaning of this phrase. The designation that a patient's care has become "futile" is commonly used to deny care to a person with a debilitating or terminal disease on the grounds that a physician or medical provider believes further medical care to be useless (see Q. 59).

Grace. The free and unmerited assistance that God gives us to respond to his call to become children of God and his adoptive sons and daughters. By grace we are born of God, and grace alone makes us real and formal participants in the intimate life of God and gives us eternal life.

Happiness. In relation to human beings, happiness is the vision of God, participation in his divine nature, and eternal joy and rest in him. As such, it is not possible in this lifetime on earth. Human beings may, however, attain imperfect happiness in this lifetime through the proper exercise of reason and the natural virtues of wisdom, courage, moderation, justice, friendship, and the like (see QQ. 80–83).

Health-care agent. A person designated to make health-care decisions for another when that person cannot make such decisions for himself (see QQ. 109–10, 116–19).

Human condition. As used in this book, this term refers the state of human beings on earth, who are ordered toward eternal life with God, but who presently live in a fallen and disordered world that tempts a person to deny his condition by avoiding evil and suffering at all costs (see QQ. 77–79).

Hydration and nutrition. Hydration and nutrition are terms for water and food, basic nonmedical necessities of life, without which anyone would die (see QQ. 15–17).

Image of God. A representation or likeness of God. Man is made in the image of God, and for this reason he possesses the dignity of a person; intellect, by which he is capable of understanding; and free will, by which he can choose between good and evil (see Q. 74).

Imminent death. A medical determination that death will happen very soon (see Q. 14).

Inevitable death. A medical determination that death cannot be prevented by further medical interventions (see Q. 14).

Intention. An act of the will proposed by the mind that forms the reason for acting (see Q. 100).

Last will and testament. A legal document, created while a person is still living, that indicates the manner in which the creator, or testator, sets forth his intention regarding the distribution of his assets at death (see Q. 112).

Living will. A legal document that is intended to convey a person's directions about end-of-life care treatment and procedures (see Q. 110).

Medical power of attorney. A legal document that appoints a health-care agent to make health-care decisions in the event of the person's incapacitation (see Q. 109).

Moral law. The rule of human conduct, whether known by reason or revelation (see QQ. 89–91).

Morality. The relation between the acts of human beings and their ultimate end. Since, for Christians, the ultimate end of man is his eternal happiness in God, morality dictates that a human act is either good or bad, as it either leads to or detracts from a person's reaching his goal of eternal life with Christ in heaven (see QQ. 84–86, 96).

Natural law. A rule of right and wrong infused at creation into the heart of every person. It contains only those duties that come from human nature and can be known by reason (see QQ. 90–91).

Neurological criteria. The condition of irreversible cessation of all functions of the entire brain, including the brain stem, as used to determine when death occurs (see Q. 38).

Ordinary and proportionate. Medical treatments or interventions that offer a reasonable hope of benefit and do not entail an excessive burden or impose excessive expense on a patient (see Q. 9).

Organ donation. The bequest of one's organs after death to help the sick and advance public health (see Q. 123).

Pain. The body's experience of physical discomfort (see Q. 61).

Palliative care. Specialized medical care that provides relief from pain and discomfort (see Q. 32).

Persistent vegetative state. A patient's condition of deep unconsciousness in which there is a complete unawareness of the self and the environment, which typically persists for six months or more (see Q. 23).

Physician–assisted suicide. Suicide with the assistance of a physician. It is also euphemistically called "medically assisted death" or "medical aid in dying" and occurs when a physician facilitates a patient's death by providing the necessary means or information to enable the patient to commit suicide (see Q. 43).

Principle of double effect. A system in Catholic moral thought to help discern the rightness or wrongness of actions that will have both good and evil effects (see Q. 31 and Appendix I).

Proportionate. *See* Ordinary and proportionate.

Quality of life. A person's subjective sense of well-being and meaning in life (see Q. 56).

Reason. The process of the mind in its function of attaining the truth (see Q. 90).

Reasonable hope of benefit. An expectation of an objective benefit to a patient from a particular medical treatment that is grounded in medical reality, including, but not limited to, the diagnosis of the patient, the specific prognosis, and the availability, success rates, cost, and burdens of any useful medical interventions, drug regimens, and therapies (see Q. 27).

Revelation. Disclosure by God of himself and his will to humans. Revelation comes in two main forms: natural (natural law) and supernatural (Sacred Scripture and Sacred Tradition) (see Q. 91).

Rule of life. A voluntary standard in a formal structure that regulates a person's conduct for more effective spiritual growth and moral living (see Appendix II).

Sacred place. A cemetery or, in certain cases, a church or an area set aside and dedicated by the competent ecclesial authority for purposes of the interment of a person's mortal remains (see QQ. 121–22).

Salvific meaning of suffering. A teaching of the Catholic Church, based upon the Biblical writings of Saint Paul in the New Testament, that a Christian may participate in the salvific suffering of Christ through his own suffering (see Q. 63).

Soul. The immaterial and immortal aspect of a human being individually created for each person by God and infused into the body at the moment of conception (see Q. 35).

Suffering. Suffering is the reaction of a human being to pain and includes both a physical and a moral dimension (see Q. 61).

Suicide. The intentional taking of one's own life (see Q. 43).

Terminal illness. The condition of having a disease that cannot be cured or adequately treated and is reasonably expected to result in one's death. Also sometimes called an "end-stage illness or disease".

Ultimate happiness. Eternal life with God (see Q. 82).

Vale of tears. An ancient Christian phrase symbolic of the fallen world and the sorrows experienced through life (see QQ. 77, 79).

Ventilator. A machine used to help a patient breathe, also called a respirator.

Virtues (moral). Moral virtues are settled dispositions (good habits) that incline and allow their possessors to make good moral choices.

APPENDIX V

Model of "Catholic Guidelines for Health-Care Agent Appointed by Medical Power of Attorney"[1]

To My Health Care Agent:

By your agreement and in a separately executed Medical Power of Attorney, I have appointed you as my agent to make any health-care decisions for me if I become unable to make my own health-care decisions, and this fact is certified in writing by my physician.

Due to physical or mental incapacity, there may come a time when I am unable to understand, make, or communicate my health-care decisions. I am providing these GUIDELINES to give you direction in the event of such an occurrence. This document is intended to provide you with the guidance needed to implement decisions for me, particularly if my death is imminent and inevitable or if I am diagnosed as being in a persistent vegetative state, coma, or other similar medical condition where I am unable to communicate my decisions.

[1] This model document is merely a starting point and is partially adapted from a PDF titled "Combined Living Will and Health Care Power of Attorney" by the Pennsylvania Catholic Conference, available at https://www .pacatholic.org/wp-content/uploads/lwformweb.pdf. The Pennsylvania Catholic Conference is to be commended for its effort to guide health-care agents. Still, for reasons outlined in QQ. 110 and 114, the authors recommend avoiding any version of a living will or using such a title.

I recognize that civil law gives my health-care agent certain powers. These powers are always to be exercised in a manner consistent with the moral teachings of the Catholic Church.

GUIDING PRINCIPLES

I understand and believe, as a Catholic, that I may never choose to cause or hasten my death intentionally. I believe that euthanasia, whatever its motives and means, is a deliberate act of taking the life of another, whether by active intervention or by omitting an action with the intention of causing death; however, the use of palliative medicines intended to alleviate my pain is acceptable if the purpose is to reduce pain and not hasten my death. I further believe, as the Church teaches, that suicide and assisted suicide are never morally permissible; thus, neither suicide nor assisted suicide may ever be an option for me.

I am mortal, and I know that I will die. I also know that my ultimate end is to be united with God in everlasting life. Therefore, I do not desire or intend to resist death if a proposed medical treatment constitutes "disproportionate or extraordinary care" as defined by the Catholic Church. As my health-care agent, you may refuse such medical treatments if doing so is consistent with the authoritative teaching of the Catholic Church.[2] Nonetheless, I desire all medical care that is "ordinary and proportionate care" as defined by the Church.

[2] In documents such as the *Catechism of the Catholic Church, Evangelium vitae, Declaration on Euthanasia, Patients in a "Permanent" Vegetative State, Nutrition and Hydration: Moral Considerations* (The Catholic Bishops of Pennsylvania, Revised Edition, 1999), *Ethical and Religious Directives for Catholic Health Care Services,* and *Responses to Certain Questions concerning Artificial Nutrition and Hydration* (Congregation for the Doctrine of the Faith, 2007).

I ask that if I fall terminally ill, I be told so without delay in order that I might prepare myself for a holy death. If I am unable to understand, communicate, or make decisions for myself, I request that a Catholic priest be contacted to attend to my spiritual needs and administer Last Rites.

Guiding Presumptions

If:

I have a medical condition that makes my death imminent and inevitable; that is, I have an incurable and irreversible medical condition that will result in my death very soon, and my death cannot be prevented despite the introduction or continuation of medical treatment; or

If I am diagnosed as being in a persistent vegetative state, coma, or other similar medical condition where I am unable to communicate my decisions

You should *presume* in favor of providing me with nutrition and hydration, including medically assisted nutrition and hydration if they can sustain my life.[3]

You should *presume* that any act or omission that, of itself, or by intention, directly causes my death to eliminate suffering is not in keeping with my wishes. Such an error of judgment, no matter how intensely motivated

---

[3] I specifically authorize, unless revoked in a future writing signed by me, all health-care providers or other covered entities to disclose to you as my health-care agent, upon your request, any information, oral or written, regarding my physical or mental health. The information includes, but is not limited to, medical and hospital records and what is otherwise private, privileged, protected, or personal health information (such as that described or defined in the Health Insurance Portability and Accountability Act of 1996 [Public Law 104–91, 100 Stat. 1936] and the regulations promulgated thereunder and any other state or local laws and rules).

by good faith, does not change the nature of this act or omission, which must always be considered contrary to my intentions, because it is contrary to the teaching of the Catholic Church.

You should *presume* that my highest desire and aim is to live and die as a faithful Catholic and, thus, my highest desire and aim regarding my own health is that you make my health-care decisions according to the principles and authoritative teachings of the Catholic faith and what you know about my stated wishes.

SPECIFIC DIRECTIONS

I direct that, regardless of my physical or mental condition, all ordinary and proportionate care be provided to me (including medically assisted nutrition and hydration, as defined by the Church).

I direct that, in the event I am unable (even with assistance) to take food and drink orally, medically assisted nutrition and hydration be provided to me, so long as it can sustain my life. It should be discontinued if it can no longer reasonably be expected to sustain my life or when it would cause me significant physical discomfort or otherwise harm me.

I direct that I receive appropriate medication to alleviate my pain, even though the administration of such medication may indirectly hasten my death. Pain medication should never be administered with the intent of hastening my death. I should be kept as free of pain as possible so that I may die comfortably and with dignity, and in the place where I choose to die. Since a person has the right to prepare for his or her death while fully conscious, I should not be deprived of consciousness without a compelling reason that you believe to be consistent with the teachings of the Catholic Church.

INDEX

and moral certitude, 43–44
prudential judgment, 23

Kasman, Deborah L., 101
Knox, Ronald, 196
Kreeft, Peter, 192

Lasance, F. X., 194
last will and testament, 164,
    168–69, 204
laypersons' understanding of
    medical technology, 22–23
Learning the Virtues (Guardini),
    192
Leo XIII (pope), 107
Lewis, C. S., 105
life
    culture's attitudes toward,
        121–22
    gift of, 121
    as sacred, 102, 121, 139, 141
life-support measures, 142
living trusts, 164
living wills, 160, 162–63,
    165–66, 204
The Lost Art of Dying
    (Dugdale), 154, 194–95

A Map of Life (Sheed), 191
Maritain, Jacques, 126
Martin, Ralph, 197
medical care vs. basic/ordinary
    care, 55–58
medically assisted death, 84;
    See also physician-assisted
    suicide
medical power of attorney,
    160, 161–63, 166, 204
    Catholic guidelines for,
        209–13

medical treatment/intervention
    aggressive treatment, 61–62,
        199
    basic or ordinary care, 55–58,
        159, 200
    Church's guidance, 50–51
    decision-making framework,
        53–54
    and dehumanization, 24
    disproportionate/
        extraordinary treatments,
        58–60, 202, 210
    factors to consider, 51–53
    moral duties/law, 49–50, 53,
        142–43
    ordinary and proportionate,
        49, 54, 205
    patient's judgment, 60–61
mercy, false, 87–88
mercy killing, 86, 137
model document, for health-
    care agent, 209–13
modern age, worldview of, 137
moral acts
    circumstances of, 148–49
    intention of, 147–48
    "object" of, 145–46
moral categories of good and
    evil, 137
The Moral Dignity of Man
    (Bristow), 192
morality, 42–43, 204
    and conscience, 91–93
    contrasted with common
        sense, 91
    moral certitude, 43–44
moral law, 137–43, 204
moral reasoning, 143
    regarding death, 21–22
moral sense, 184–85